HOMETOWN
HARDBALL

HOMETOWN HARDBALL

TIM HEALEY

A Minor League Baseball Road Trip
from the Rocky Shores of Maine to the
Bright Lights of New York City

**Globe
Pequot**

GUILFORD, CONNECTICUT

All the information in this book is subject to change. We recommend readers call ahead
to obtain current information before traveling.

Globe Pequot

An imprint of Rowman & Littlefield

Distributed by NATIONAL BOOK NETWORK

Copyright © 2017 by Rowman & Littlefield

Copyright © 2017 by Tim Healey

British Library Cataloguing in Publication Information Available
Library of Congress Cataloging-in-Publication Data Available

ISBN 978-1-4930-2858-0 (paperback)
ISBN 978-1-4930-2859-7 (e-book)

™ The paper used in this publication meets the minimum requirements of American National Standard
for Information Sciences—Permanence of Paper for Printed Library Materials, ANSI/NISO Z39.48-1992.

To my parents, Cynthia and Gerard, who nurtured
—and then dealt with—my love of baseball.

And to Patrick, my first interview subject.

· CONTENTS ·

GEOGRAPHICAL INDEX

· INTRODUCTION ·

And they'll walk out to the bleachers, sit in their shirtsleeves on a perfect afternoon. They'll find they have reserved seats somewhere along one of the baselines, where they sat when they were children and cheered their heroes. And they'll watch the game and it'll be as if they dipped themselves in magic waters. The memories will be so thick they'll have to brush them away from their faces. People will come, Ray. The one constant through all the years, Ray, has been baseball. America has rolled by like an army of steamrollers. It has been erased like a blackboard, rebuilt, and erased again. But baseball has marked the time.

—Terrence Mann, *Field of Dreams*

It's easy to be romantic about baseball. Two teams, nine innings, three strikes, four balls, three outs—no matter where you are in the world, baseball is baseball.

The difference is in the details, and the details are what we bring you with *Hometown Hardball*. Consider this book a guide to affiliated minor league baseball stadiums in the northeast—the homes of all twenty-seven teams in the six New England states, plus New York, New Jersey, and Pennsylvania. In detailing bits about the clubs, the history, the food, the fans, the neighborhoods, and so on, we want to tell you what makes a day at one ballpark fun and different from the others.

From Portland to Brooklyn, Rochester to Williamsport, Pawtucket to Altoona, and everywhere in between, the game will be the same. But the routine and tradition in these towns, big or small, are each their own experience.

TRIPLE-A
BALLPARKS

MCCOY STADIUM

HOME OF THE
Pawtucket Red Sox

LOCATION: Pawtucket, RI

TIME FROM:

WORCESTER, MA:	50 minutes
BOSTON, MA:	1 hour
HARTFORD, CT:	1 hour, 40 minutes
PORTLAND, ME:	2 hours, 30 minutes
NEW YORK, NY:	3 hours, 30 minutes

OPENED: 1942

CAPACITY: 10,031

TENANT: Pawtucket Red Sox, Triple-A International League (1973–present)

PAST TENANTS: Pawtucket Red Sox, Double-A Eastern League (1970–72)

Pawtucket Indians, Double-A Eastern League (1966–67)

Pawtucket Slaters, Class B (1946–49)

DISTANCE FROM HOME PLATE: 325 to left and right fields, 400 feet to center

RADIO: 920 AM (Providence)

Longest Game Ever

If you're familiar with McCoy Stadium, it's probably for one of two reasons: One, it's the home of the Pawtucket Red Sox, Boston's Triple-A farm team, where the organization's top prospects often get their last reps before reaching The Show. And two, McCoy Stadium was the site of the longest game in the history of professional baseball—a thirty-three-inning affair in 1981 between the PawSox and Rochester Red Wings that started on April 18 and ended on June 23.

The contest is immortalized in a book, *Bottom of the 33rd: Hope, Redemption, and Baseball's Longest Game*, by the *New York Times*' Dan Barry, but here's the short version: The PawSox and Red Wings played thirty-two innings, starting April 18 and ending at 4:09 a.m. April 19—Easter Sunday. International League president Harold Cooper suspended the game. The teams had been playing for seven hours.

The game resumed two months later with the thirty-third—and ultimately final—inning. It was broadcast on national TV, due in part to the Major League Baseball strike, and took only eighteen minutes to wrap up. Dave Koza singled to left field to score Marty Barrett. The PawSox won 3-2. The final statistics: 882 pitches in eight hours and twenty-five minutes. Future Hall of Famer Cal Ripken, Jr., playing for Rochester, had fifteen plate appearances. The teams struck out a combined sixty times in 219 at-bats.

The Longest Game offers a window into the franchise's rich history. The PawSox, who adopted their parent team's name in 1970, have long served as a preview of what's to come in Boston, an hour away. Think of any homegrown Red

Free Tom Brady!

One of the team's first promotions in 2016 was a Free Tom Brady night, during which anybody named Tom or Brady got in for free. The normally $13 tickets were reduced to $12 in honor of the famed Patriots quarterback's jersey number.

Sox player from the last half-century or so—including core members of the World Series–winning teams in 2007 and 2013—and there is a good chance he made a stop in Pawtucket. In fact, about three out of every four players to play for the PawSox have reached the majors at some point.

The Little Brother

If you visit McCoy Stadium, do so for the history and tradition more than for the perks or amenities of the ballpark. It's not uncommon in recent years for teams to build souped-up state-of-the-art facilities to attract fans (or for towns to build them to attract teams), but the PawSox do not have one of those in McCoy.

McCoy was built in 1942 (though it received renovations around the turn of the century) and looks it. A World War II–era utilitarian bowl of concrete, the stadium is not especially attractive and it is located in a not especially attractive neighborhood. All is not lost, however. If you're spending a day or weekend in the area, Providence, the state's capital, has its good side and is only fifteen minutes down the road—and again, Boston is only an hour away.

The PawSox are trying to change, though. When new ownership took over the team in 2014, one of its first moves was an effort to move the team to a new stadium in Providence. That project never got off the ground, however, and in late 2015 the team brought in three new executives—Chairman Larry Lucchino, President Dr. Charles Steinberg, and General Manager Dan Rea III—to rejuvenate the organization and do damage control on what had become a major public relations debacle. Lucchino and Steinberg are veterans of the Red Sox front office that revamped Fenway Park in the mid-2000s, and the hope is they will do the same in Pawtucket. As of early 2017, the PawSox were looking at potential sites for a new stadium in and around Pawtucket, with the long-term fate of McCoy remaining up in the air.

One of their specialties includes goings-on related to fans' in-game experiences. Among their quick fixes was replacing the old net behind home plate with one that has thinner wires, thus making it easier to see. They also re-did a barbeque area down the first-base line that is exclusive to group outings during the pregame but open to general-admission ticket holders during the game and offers a great view. The new front office also worked with the city to add new "This Way to McCoy Stadium" signs all over the neighborhood, which are rather helpful to those unfamiliar with old, winding New England roads. The benefit to McCoy is that it is logistically very simple, just a couple minutes off I-95 and with plenty of on-site parking. There are also private off-site lots in the neighborhood for when McCoy's fill up.

The PawSox's goal is, as Steinberg put it, to be the little brother to the big brother in Boston.

Have a Seat

McCoy Stadium isn't sexy, but one of the main tenets of minor league baseball remains true there: There isn't a bad seat in the place. The main seating bowl is divided into three sections—green closest to the field, red above that, then a ring of blue up highest—and almost all of it is covered by an overhang that protects fans from spring rain and summer heat. In the outfield, there is a section of bleachers in right field and a grassy berm in left, similar to the outfield at JetBlue Park, the Red Sox's spring training home.

The PawSox, as a Triple-A team, play at the highest of the six levels of the minor leagues. The majors are sixty minutes and a world away. Pawtucket's roster is consistently a mix of career minor leaguers hoping to get one more shot—or maybe their first shot—in the bigs and young prospects being groomed to support the parent club. Since they broke through with a World Series win in 2004, the Red Sox have consistently had one of the best farm systems in baseball, which means a regular supply of some of the most exciting young minor leaguers in the country calling McCoy home.

Basic Fare

Food-wise, McCoy offers traditional ballpark fare, including ice cream for when it's hot and hot chocolate for when it's not.

See Them Now

The best part about McCoy: seeing the Red Sox stars of tomorrow. The players could quite literally end up in Boston any day.

Take Junichi Tazawa as an example. A bullpen mainstay before, during, and after the club's 2013 World Series championship, Tazawa was once just a major league hopeful, one in a long line of Next Big Things working on his craft in Pawtucket. As fans arrived at McCoy on August 7, 2009, he was one of the main draws. News spread that evening, however, that nobody in Rhode Island was going to see Tazawa that night. He wasn't even there. The Red Sox called him up, and he had to rush off to the Bronx. The PawSox beat Norfolk without him, and Tazawa made his major league debut in the 14th inning of an eventual loss to the Yankees.

Fishing for Autographs

"Watch and learn" is an organizing principle for much of life on this planet, and it's no different for many of the more than 17 million people who have visited McCoy Stadium in the last four decades. At McCoy, built during World War II and tucked into a mostly residential neighborhood in working-class Pawtucket, autograph seekers have a method as unusual as any you'll see in a baseball setting, a method with no obvious origin but a very clear objective.

At minor league parks across the country, the autograph-obtaining routine is, well, routine. Fans crowd around a specific corner of the

park, usually near the dugouts or where there is a lot of player foot traffic in the hopes that some of them will stop and oblige with a signature. Also popular is waiting outside the stadium after a game to catch players as they head to their cars or the team bus.

McCoy Stadium is different. There are no field-level seats aside from a handful of luxury boxes, so the sections closest to play are above the dugouts. Fans are a bit more removed from the players' environment, and fan-player interaction is more difficult to achieve.

Generations of McCoy attendees have worked around this, however. In the hour before and minutes after each game, fans "fish" for autographs near the home and away dugouts. They use some sort of container—a red Solo cup, a bisected one-gallon milk jug, a plastic pumpkin meant for Halloween candy, anything—and tie a string around it. Then they put their baseball, program, photos, cards, or other item of choice in the container and carefully drop it over a railing. The pseudo-fishing rods, bait and all, hang there by the edge of the dugout and warning-track dirt. Kids wait to see if they get any bites.

"It's a way for them to touch you without being next to you," said Rich Gedman, a New England and baseball lifer.

Gedman has witnessed this fishing custom for decades. After growing up in nearby Worcester, Massachusetts, he signed with the Red Sox in 1977, weeks shy of his eighteenth birthday. He spent the end of that summer practicing—and watching and learning—with the PawSox at McCoy. By the time first pitch arrived each night, Gedman transitioned to the seats to watch with everybody else. Within those first few days, it struck him: Huh. This is different.

Past Greats

Here's a partial look at some noteworthy big leaguers who made stops in Pawtucket before their major league successes:

1970s:

Carlton Fisk, Jim Rice, Tony Conigliaro

1980s:

Wade Bogs, Roger Clemens, Dennis "Oil Can" Boyd, Rich Gedman, Mike Greenwell, Bobby Ojeda

1990s:

Nomar Garciaparra, Derek Lowe, Lou Merloni, Trot Nixon, Jason Varitek, Mo Vaughn

2000s:

Bronson Arroyo, Clay Buchholz, Jacoby Ellsbury, Jon Lester, Justin Masterson, Jonathan Papelbon, Dustin Pedroia, Josh Reddick, Kevin Youkilis

2010s:

Mookie Betts, Xander Bogaerts, Jackie Bradley, Jr., Brock Holt, Eduardo Rodriguez, Travis Shaw, Blake Swihart, Junichi Tazawa

"You don't see it very often. You're close, but you're not close," Gedman said of the odd seating setup. "It seemed like it was something that the fans just always did."

Gedman reached McCoy again in 1980, this time making his last stop on the minor league ladder en route to a decade-long career as an All-Star catcher with the Boston Red Sox. More than thirty years after that, Gedman—with his three children grown and out of the house—returned to Pawtucket as the team's hitting coach.

Years passed. Thousands of fans and hundreds of players came and went. But there Gedman was again, at McCoy, with fans fishing for autographs, a tradition as steady as the national pastime itself.

"You see major league balls, you see little league balls, you see balls that have been used, you see balls that are brand new," Gedman said. "Books. Baseball cards. Whatever you have. It doesn't have to be anything special."

Players can benefit from McCoy's fishing tradition, too. Sox coach Rich Gedman pointed out that it's not as personal as the physical exchange of ball and pen between fan and player, but it's not difficult for athletes like Blake Swihart to find the positive side.

The Red Sox made Swihart their first-round draft pick in June 2011, attaching to the athletic catcher from New Mexico a certain degree of fame and expectation that comes with being selected so early. Everywhere Swihart went in his journey to the majors—from Greenville, South Carolina, to Salem, Virginia, to Portland, Maine—he was among the most popular targets of Sharpie-wielding fans.

Those sorts of situations can become hairy. It's typically a good-natured moment—"You try to make someone's day," as Gedman puts it—

but when there are too many fans to satisfy, or the occasional awkwardly aggressive adult, it can be difficult for players to extricate themselves from the pack to get back to work.

The fishing routine helps that. It's a much more passive activity, and if players have a spare moment or two they can go down the line and sign however many items they want. "It's a lot better than getting hounded," said Swihart. "It's a lot easier and you're not feeling overwhelmed. You're almost more willing to do it. I've never seen anything like it before. It's kind of cool, the tradition. I know they've been doing it forever."

FRONTIER FIELD

HOME OF THE
Rochester Red Wings

LOCATION:	Rochester, NY
TIME FROM:	
BUFFALO, NY:	1 hour, 15 minutes
SYRACUSE, NY:	1 hour, 20 minutes
TORONTO, CANADA:	2 hours, 45 minutes
ALBANY, NY:	3 hours, 30 minutes
SPRINGFIELD, MA:	4 hours, 30 minutes
NEW YORK, NY:	5 hours, 30 minutes
OPENED:	1997
CAPACITY:	13,500
TENANT:	Rochester Red Wings, Triple-A International League (1997–present)
PAST TENANTS:	None
DISTANCE FROM HOME PLATE:	335 feet to left field, 402 to center, 322 to right
RADIO:	1280 AM (Rochester)

Lovin' the Ripkens

Rochester is similar to Cincinnati in that it is not necessarily a destination city, but a legitimate city nonetheless with a proud baseball tradition. The history of Frontier Field is relatively short, with the Red Wings celebrating their twentieth season here in 2016. The history of professional baseball in Rochester, however, is a long and august one.

Rochester's first pro team formed in 1877 (that's not a typo). Since then, the Rochester Hustlers/Bronchos/Tribe/Jingoes/Brownies/ Colts have played in the International Association, New York State League, American Association, Eastern Association, and Eastern League, among others. Most of that happened when professional baseball lacked stability and saw teams and leagues come into and out of existence within years. In 1928, Rochester adopted the Red Wings moniker. It's been that way ever since.

As far as high-profile minor league games go, Frontier Field didn't have to wait long. The

Before Baseball

While the Red Wings didn't call Frontier Field home until 1997, construction finished in 1996. The first event it hosted was a Beach Boys concert on July 12, 1996. The next night, Frontier Field hosted its first sporting event, a soccer match between the Rochester Raging Rhinos and the Montreal Impact.

Red Wings hosted their then-parent team, the Baltimore Orioles, for an exhibition on July 10, 1997, during Major League Baseball's All-Star break. Later that year, they won the International League's Governor's Cup (as they did again in 2006). In 2000, Frontier Field hosted the Triple-A All-Star Game, televised nationally on ESPN2.

Another aspect of Rochester worth knowing is that Rochesterians love them some Ripkens. Cal Sr. was a player (1961) and manager (1969–70), while sons Cal Jr. and Billy both played (1981 and 1987 respectively). Cal Jr., as the most successful of the bunch, both while in Rochester and in the major leagues, is the most popular.

"He's one of Rochester's favorite sons," says Red Wings boss Dan Mason. "Our people have adopted him and called him our own. He was as big a star in major league baseball as there was at the time."

Old-School Charm

If you visit Frontier Field and it feels like a scaled-down version of the Baltimore Orioles' Camden Yards, that's okay—more than okay, even. That's what the Red Wings were going for when they were an O's affiliate planning the park two decades ago.

Like Camden Yards, widely considered one of the nicest stadiums in the majors, Frontier Field is a newer building that seamlessly blends into a long-existent neighborhood in the heart of downtown Rochester. From the outside, it has an old-school feel to it, not shiny or modern like more recently erected places. The bricks used to construct Frontier were selected because they looked like bricks in the older, surrounding buildings. The immediate neighborhood includes lots of factories—whose empty lots serve as relatively inexpensive Red Wings parking—but beyond that a block or two it gives way to a more downtown feel.

The upkeep is constant—painting this and fixing that, adding new seats or maintaining

A New Perspective

Once the weather warms, you are excused if your eyes are drawn away from the action and toward the buildings beyond Frontier during night games. Rochester has a sneaky-gorgeous skyline, including the distinct Kodak Tower, and Frontier Field is one of the best places from which to take it in. That dawned on Mason, a Rochester-area lifer, one night twenty years ago when the new park was still under construction.

"I was here tying up some lose ends," Mason said. "I looked up and I'm like, 'That's pretty dang cool.' I never realized we had a cool skyline until that night."

a general-admission section. Mason, who has been the Red Wings' general manager since 1995 and is a de facto local celebrity, compared Frontier Field to a baby.

"You see your son or your daughter get older and go through different stages, and that's what it was like when Frontier Field was being built," Mason said. "We don't want it to look like a twenty-year-old facility. We want people to walk into this place and say 'wow.'"

As soon as you step inside, the clean and modern amenities do away with any skepticism the old-timey façade might induce. Frontier Field even has free Wi-Fi—a benefit, one might assume, to selling your stadium name rights to a leading telecommunications company.

The seating options are fairly straightforward. The lower bowl is surrounded by a con-

Looking Down

In Rochester, the playing field itself is set into the ground below street level, so when you walk in through the front gate you end up looking *down* on the field. It's unusual, but feels right—and definitely limits the number of stairs you'll need to climb to get to any particular seat.

course, which is surrounded by an upper bowl. Frontier Field feels spacious, not cramped, and that's especially true near the grassy berm areas down the left- and right-field lines (in foul territory). There are group-type areas in left and right fields, though it's mostly for pregame eating and mingling before fans head to the seats come game time.

Low-Key Americana

Since the Red Wings play at the Triple-A level, the quality of play should be pretty high—as good as it gets without watching the majors.

Like lots of other minor league teams, though, the level of play is oftentimes secondary to those running the show. The Red Wings try to make sure there is a lot going on aside from the game, and in an effort to lure all sorts of people to the park, they bring in a variety of celebrities. Some have local connections (former Bills quarterback Jim Kelly), some are low-key American heroes (Mike Eruzione of "Miracle on Ice" fame), and some are former baseball superstars (all-time hit king Pete Rose). Consider it well-meaning bait. "Give them a taste of what Frontier Field is about," Mason says. "And hopefully get them hooked. Once they see what it's like, [they] fall in love and come back again."

Like other minor league towns in New York and Pennsylvania, Rochester is an old industrial city. One remnant of that is old (but active) train tracks beyond right field. Trains of the freight and passenger varieties go by several times per game, reminiscent of the subway at the old Yankee Stadium, and engineers usually appease onlookers with a honk of the loud train horn. Cheers ensue.

If you visit Rochester, maybe wait until June or so. Early-season games can be brutal weather-wise. How brutal? Consider that in recent years, the Red Wings have advertised a "50-degree guarantee," meaning that if temperatures don't reach 50 degrees on opening day, fans in attendance can redeem that ticket stub for any other April or May home game. In 2016, the team even had to postpone opening day be-

Ballpark Eats

Frontier Field is known for its food—so much so, according to Mason, that fans like to come hungry. "You can come to seventy-two home games," he says, "and have a different entrée every game." Here is a sampling of the options:

Say Cheese! with specialty/custom-made mac and cheese

Red Osier, a local eatery known for its roast beef and prime rib

Black Angus Grill

Big Red BBQ

Altobelli Deli

If you *don't* want to show up hungry, check out Rocky's House, a Rochester landmark and family-owned Italian joint only a five-minute walk away.

cause temperatures only reached 29 degrees. When the Red Wings played the next day, temperatures didn't come close to 50, and fans went home with free tickets for another game.

Number 8,222

In nine decades of Red Wings baseball, and nearly a century and a half of Rochester baseball, the team and city have retired only three numbers. Each number, as well as the last name and a photo of the person each honors, is painted on the wall in left-center field, plain for all to see.

The pseudo-mural seems straightforward at first. Number 26, for Joe Altobelli, Rochester's "Mr. Baseball" who at different times served as a player, coach, manager, general manager, and radio color commentator; Number 36, for Luke Easter, who finished a long professional career as a Red Wings slugger in the early 1960s; and Number 8,222, for Rochester businessman Morrie Silver.

Wait, what? Number 8,222? Silver is as significant a figure as any in Red Wings lore, and it's with good reason that pieces of the neighborhood—including the old Silver Stadium and One Morrie Silver Way, Frontier Field's actual address—carry his name. Silver, a Rochester music store owner and real estate developer in the 1950s, saved Rochester baseball in the winter of 1956 to 1957.

The St. Louis Cardinals, at the time the Red Wings' owner, wanted to sell the club. New owners always means a potential move, and to Silver and others in the community the thought of losing the Red Wings was unbearable. Silver spearheaded a stock drive in which locals

purchased shares of the team, collectively taking legal ownership of a team they always sentimentally owned anyway. In all, 8,222 shares were bought—some people buying a hundred, many buying just one or two. The Red Wings' quirky claim to fame is that No. 8,222 is the highest retired number in professional sports.

Come spring of 1957, the Red Wings played under new—and stable—ownership, that of Rochester Community Baseball, Inc., which purchased the club from the Cardinals for $500,000. The stock drive is known as the 72-day Miracle.

Past Greats

Here's a partial look at some noteworthy big leaguers who played at Frontier Field. It's worth noting that some of the best former Red Wings—a lengthy list that includes Brady Anderson, Don Baylor, Bob Gibson, Tim McCarver, Jamie Moyer, Stan Musial, Mike Mussina, Curt Schilling, and Cal Ripken, Jr.—made their Rochester stops before Frontier Field existed, and thus aren't on this list.

1990s:
Sidney Ponson

2000s:
Michael Cuddyer, Matt Garza, Justin Morneau, Jason Kubel, Joe Mauer, Pat Neshek

2010s:
Brian Dozier, Wilson Ramos, Danny Valencia

"The fact that we're literally owned by our community is different," said Mason. "Community is our middle name."

Shares of Rochester Community Baseball today, more than a half-century removed from that initial and only offering organized by Silver, are not sold or publicly traded. They are sometimes passed down when a relative dies, and occasionally change hands between friends. About 200 shareholders remain.

The unusual ownership dynamic doesn't result in any sort of significant difference in day-to-day team activities compared to a more routine setup. A board oversees business decisions, and every January the team hosts a shareholders meetings—an excuse, essentially, for the Red Wings' biggest fans to get together in the middle of the winter and chat about Rochester and baseball. Usually there is a state-of-the-organization type of presentation from the chairman of the board, and the field manager comes to town for a Q&A session.

The plus side to effectively having no lone owner to whom to respond is that the financial bottom line isn't really the bottom line at all. Rochester Community Baseball does not pay dividends. Pure profit is not the main motivation, and although the Red Wings need to make money—to pay staff, rent the stadium from Monroe County, etc.—they're able to keep ticket and concession prices down because of it.

The lighthearted downside to effectively having no lone owner is that Mason and other Red Wings executives have a whole bunch of people to whom to respond.

"I have a lot of bosses," Mason says, laughing. "There are people all over I run into every day who say, 'Oh, I have two shares,' or 'I have

one share.' So it's pretty cool that we have people who feel a special tie to the team, because they own part of the team. . . . Not many people in the country can say they own a team or part of a team."

History Lesson

Rochester hero Morrie Silver died in 1974, but his legacy lives on. He's in the International League Hall of Fame, and was a member of the inaugural Red Wings Hall of Fame class in 1989. Silver's widow, Anna Bert Silver, was a Chairman of the Board in the 1980s. Silver's daughter, Naomi Silver, is still very much involved with the team and in the community. She started as an intern in 1988 and is now the president, CEO, and COO.

Outside Frontier Field stands a larger-than-life statue of Morrie Silver and a child. The bronze figures, commissioned by sculptor Dejan Pejovic, were dedicated in a July 2007 ceremony and serve at once as a memorial and a history lesson for all who visit. The model of the child depicted, it turns out, is a grandson Silver never met. His name is Morrie, too.

COCA-COLA FIELD

HOME OF THE
Buffalo Bisons

LOCATION: Buffalo, NY

TIME FROM:

ROCHESTER, NY:	1 hour, 15 minutes
ERIE, PA:	1 hour, 30 minutes
TORONTO, Canada:	1 hour, 45 minutes
CLEVELAND, OH:	3 hours
PITTSBURGH, PA:	3 hours, 15 minutes
DETROIT, MI:	4 hours
ALBANY, NY:	4 hours, 15 minutes
NEW YORK, NY:	6 hours

OPENED: 1988

CAPACITY: 16,907

TENANT: Buffalo Bisons, Triple-A American Association (1988–97) and Triple-A International League (1998–present)

DISTANCE FROM HOME PLATE: 325 feet to left and right fields, 404 to center

RADIO: 1520 AM (Buffalo)

New(est) Era

In the long history of Buffalo professional baseball, many dates can serve as an entry point. You can start in 1877, when the original Buffalo Bisons played their first season, or in 1879, when they played in the National League. Or you can go to 1886, when the Bisons joined the minors. To skip over those early years from which records are iffy, jump ahead to 1979, when baseball returned to Buffalo after an eight-year absence. And then there is 1985, when the Bisons moved back to Triple-A.

But for our purposes, let's start in 1988, when Coca-Cola Field debuted to a jam-packed crowd of 19,500 people.

Buffalo, with the NFL's Bills and NHL's Sabres already calling the city home, tried to entice a Major League Baseball team, too, by building a new stadium. With an original capacity of 19,500, Coca-Cola Field—then Pilot Field—was constructed in such a way that the city would have been able to add a second deck relatively easily in the event that its MLB dreams came true.

Alas, they did not. The larger (and warmer) locales of Tampa Bay, Phoenix, Miami, and Washington, D.C., all won teams over the course of the next two decades. (So did Denver, which is larger but not necessarily warmer.)

Grammar Lesson

For the pedants among us: Even though the plural form of bison is bison, Buffalo's baseball team is indeed the Bisons, with an s at the end. It's been that way since the first Buffalo Bisons team in the late 1800s, and the original reason why seems to be lost to history.

Oh, and another thing about Bisons: Buffalonians pronounce the s as a soft z. So a phonetic spelling would be Bizons. Yeah, it's weird.

a player to the big league team or when Blue Jays player-development people want to pop down to see their prospects.

The Bisons estimate that about 25 percent of their individual ticket sales are from Canadians, more than double the pre–Blue Jays mark. When the Jays do well, as was the case when it qualified for the American League Championship Series in 2015 and 2016, it's especially common to see Toronto merchandise in the stands at Bisons games (even though Buffalo is predominantly a Yankees town). The parent team does a fair amount of promoting for the Bisons, too, so as to remind their fans that, hey, the Blue Jays of tomorrow are playing not too far away. The Jays' flagship radio station, Sportsnet 590 The FAN, broadcasts a dozen or so Bisons games every summer.

Buffalo doesn't really harbor MLB hopes anymore, but instead has become a Triple-A landmark. Coca-Cola Field fits nearly 17,000 people now—more later on the drop in capacity—the largest of any minor league baseball stadium in the country. The Bisons dominate the all-time single-season minor league attendance leaderboards, with 1991 coming in at number one thanks to 1,240,951 fans.

The Bisons have switched affiliations a few times in recent decades, from the Pittsburgh Pirates (1988–94) to the Cleveland Indians (1995–2008) to the New York Mets (2009–12) to, now, the Toronto Blue Jays (2013–present).

The latest partnership works spectacularly. Coca-Cola Field is a little over an hour and a half from Toronto's Rogers Centre, simplifying logistics when the Blue Jays need to promote

Have a Seat

About that decreasing seating capacity: Coca-Cola Park peaked at 21,050 people maximum but is down to fewer than 17,000—with more incremental drops likely in the coming years—due to renovations the Bisons have done each offseason.

Again, Buffalo was thinking big when it birthed the ballpark in the mid-1980s. Those MLB hopes have long faded, however, leaving the Bisons with a whole lot of stadium. They average more than 8,000 fans per game—a solid number—but that still leaves about half of Coca-Cola Field empty.

So, as they remove old seats, the Bisons are installing new ones that are wider and more comfortable, helping Coca-Cola Field keep up with its younger league-mates. Also helping that endeavor: A video board 80 feet wide and 33 feet high, the largest of its kind when the Bisons added it in 2011.

The stadium's main bowl includes two levels and price points, split from third base to first base by a walkway. That walkway ends, though, so for the sections that stretch from the out-field grass to the foul poles, you need to use the closed concourse to access your seat. The left-field corner of the main bowl has general-admission seating. The upper deck is a mix of luxury suites and regular seating.

Coca-Cola Field features several group areas. The Labatt Blue Zone, a two-tier par-ty area, is behind first base. You can rent out the entire space or one of the levels. The Bully Hill Party Deck, a three-tier group section, is in right field. It neighbors a grassy berm, which serves as a spillover zone between Bully Hill and a center-field party pavilion used mostly for pregame goings-on.

Another draw is Pettibones Grille, a restau-rant space along the first-base line that special-

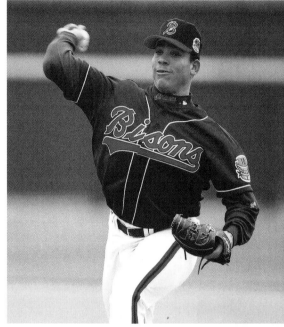

Local Legend

In at least one way, 2016 was the end of an era for Coca-Cola Field. Larry Owens, better known to Bisons fans as "the Peanut Man," died in October. He was seventy-one.

Owens was the first person the Bisons hired before Coca-Cola Park opened in 1988, and for more than a quarter-century he dished out pea-nuts—regular, salted, and Cajun—to fans on the concourse by Section 104.

izes in group get-togethers—office meetings, holiday parties, etc.—year-round, but during Bisons season opens up two hours before first pitch for regular folks to have dinner.

The Bisons play in downtown Buffalo, so parking can be a tricky. The team doesn't own any lots. A bunch of privately owned options are within walking distance, and there is public transportation that drops you off right at Coca-Cola Field.

The upside to being downtown is the eat/drink/hotel options, including Pearl Street Grill & Brewery two blocks away. That section of Buffalo has allegedly undergone a bit of a resurgence in recent years, and more and more people are living there, too.

Hello, Neighbor

The Bisons' season starts in early April. The Buffalo Sabres, who play at the KeyBank Center a ten-minute walk away, don't end their regular season until mid-April, so there is almost always at least some overlap.

When both teams play at home on the same night—or when there is a concert or another major event at the multi-purpose KeyBank Center—it can make for a busy neighborhood.

It can make parking more of a hassle, sure, but the real challenge is the stretching of the stadiums and concessions personnel. The Bisons and Sabres use the same company to staff their facilities.

Fri-yay

One Buffalo Bisons tradition is as old as Coca-Cola Field itself. For nearly three decades, they have held the Friday Night Bash every Friday home game, when they open the gates early for batting practice and happy hour, complete with food and drink specials. There is always a theme—'70s Night, Top Gun Night, Zombie Night—and a postgame fireworks show.

The largest fireworks show every year, though, is so big that the Bisons brand it with capital letters, the Largest Fireworks Show of the Season. It happens every July 3 during the team's "Independence Eve" celebration. The Buffalo Philharmonic Orchestra and Chorus plays a concert after the game and before the colorful explosives light up the sky.

One other Bisons mainstay worth noting is their mascot race, the Chicken Wing Race with its four contestants: Chicken Wing, Atomic Wing, Bleu Cheese, and Celery. Poor Celery has never won.

Past Greats

Here's a partial look at some noteworthy big leaguers who played at Coca-Cola Field.

1990s:

Moises Alou, Jeff Banister, Sean Casey, Terry Collins (manager), Bartolo Colon, Brian Giles, Dave Roberts, Marco Scutaro, Richie Sexson, Tim Wakefield

2000s:

Milton Bradley, Asdrubal Cabrera, Shin-Soo Choo, Coco Crisp, Travis Hafner, Cliff Lee, Victor Martinez, Jon Niese, Jhonny Peralta, Brandon Phillips, Grady Sizemore, Eric Wedge (manager)

2010s:

Lucas Duda, Jeurys Familia, Matt Harvey, Daniel Murphy, Kevin Pillar, Aaron Sanchez, Marcus Stroman, Devon Travis, Zack Wheeler

The Many Minor Leagues

The phrase "minor leagues" is a bit of a catchall. There are actually fourteen domestic minor leagues spread across five levels (or more, counting subdivisions). It's normal for a player to take a half-decade or longer to climb the ladder—if he finishes climbing the ladder at all.

Here is a rundown of the four leagues in the northeast, the ones with teams featured in this book.

INTERNATIONAL LEAGUE (TRIPLE A)

"International" is a bit of a misnomer—there aren't any Canadian clubs left—but IL teams compete at the highest level of the minor leagues. Triple-A rosters are filled largely with older players hoping to get another (or a first) shot at life in the bigs, with a few of younger prospects mixed in.

EASTERN LEAGUE (DOUBLE A)

Triple A and Double A constitute the "upper minors," the last rungs on the ladder before The Show. Major league general managers commonly consider a player a realistic potential call-up (if a need arises) once he reaches the Eastern League. Some of baseball's best prospects jump straight from the EL to the parent team.

SOUTH ATLANTIC LEAGUE (LOW A)

Single A is split into High A and Low A. The South Atlantic League—or Sally League—is the latter and has one team in the northeast, the Lakewood Blue Claws (formerly of Fayetteville, North Carolina). The majors are a ways away for players in the Sally League, but you have to start somewhere.

NEW YORK–PENN LEAGUE (SHORT-SEASON A)

The NYPL is a "short-season" league, meaning they start in mid-June and end around early September. It's one of the lowest rungs on the ladder, and rosters are filled with recent draftees and teenagers. It's common to see a major league team assign its top draft pick each summer to its NYPL affiliate.

NBT BANK STADIUM

HOME OF THE
Syracuse Chiefs

LOCATION:	Syracuse, NY
TIME FROM:	
ROCHESTER, NY:	1 hour, 30 minutes
ALBANY, NY:	2 hours, 15 minutes
TORONTO, Canada:	3 hours, 45 minutes
HARTFORD, CT:	3 hours, 45 minutes
PHILADELPHIA, PA:	4 hours
NEW YORK, NY:	4 hours
BOSTON, MA:	4 hours, 30 minutes
OPENED:	1997
CAPACITY:	11,731
TENANT:	Syracuse Chiefs, Triple-A International League (1997–present)
DISTANCE FROM HOME PLATE:	330 feet to left and right fields, 400 feet to center
RADIO:	1260 AM (Syracuse)

Longtime Home

The history of the Syracuse Chiefs, which dates back to 1876 as a professional franchise and to 1934 as an affiliated minor league team, is a storied one. The current club came to town in the early 1960s, when a group of prominent locals, including future general manager Tex Simone and then-mayor Anthony Henninger, rallied to form the Community Baseball Club of Central New York, Inc.

That private organization, split into shares owned by about 4,000 individuals, bought the Montreal Royals after the 1960 season and moved them to Syracuse for 1961. It remains the Chiefs' owner, and a board of directors serves as the decision-makers. The setup is similar to Rochester's, though the Chiefs don't seem to make it a central part of their identity like the Red Wings do. General manager Jason Smorol said about 80 percent of shareholders own just one share.

The Syracuse Chiefs are coming out of a down stretch—hopefully. The board of directors opted for a hard reset after 2013, when attendance plummeted to its lowest point since NBT Bank Stadium opened in 1997. The Simones—Tex, who was general manager from 1970 through 1996, and his son John, who served in the same role from 1997 through 2013—were done. The board installed Smorol as GM.

The regime change has yielded slow progress, but progress nonetheless. Attendance in 2016 was 4,158 fans per game, up from 3,743 in 2013. The team is losing less money than it did under previous leadership. And, as the second most popular sporting event in the city behind Syracuse University men's basketball, the Chiefs are trying to be more of a presence outside the ballpark and around town. "We're changing culture of the Chiefs in community," Smorol said.

Have a Seat

NBT Bank Stadium is a whole lot of ballpark, with a legitimate upper deck bookending the press/suite level, but attendance in recent years has left something to be desired. To help account for that, the team "rightsized" the joint in advance of the 2016 season, covering five sections—three in left, two in right—in the upper deck with tarp.

Attendance overall is trending upward, a positive and logical development considering NBT is a decent stadium with plenty of quality seating options.

The main bowl has two levels split by a walkway. Premium field box seats are on the first level, stretching to about the outer edge of the infield dirt on both sides. Reserved box seating bookends those premium spots—just

Family Legacy

The Simones no longer run the Syracuse Chiefs, but they still have a presence in and around NBT Bank Stadium. The ballpark's address is 1 Tex Simone Drive, and in the Hank Sauer Room—a VIP space of sorts down the right-field line—sits a bronze bust of Tex, who was instrumental in bringing to Syracuse the latest iteration of the Chiefs in 1961. Tex passed away in 2015.

about reaching the foul poles—and continues throughout the second level.

The upper deck consists now of six sections of reserved seating, but the real draw up there are the group sections. On either end of the 300-level suites are patios, more or less open, outdoor areas for groups. On either end of the 400-level suites are terraces, which are smaller patios.

The Chiefs have centralized the rest of their group sections to the right-field corner. The Hank Sauer Room is a premium option and is sometimes used for specialty events, such as a Mother's Day brunch. It neighbors a picnic area. The Party Deck, new in late 2015, is a wooden deck sometimes reserved for groups and sometimes open to everybody. It overlooks right field and is the only spot in the park where you can catch home runs.

Parking is abundant. The old MacArthur Stadium, home to the Chiefs' from 1934 until 1996, was demolished and is now a parking lot.

Smorol half-jokingly said the ballpark is ten minutes from anywhere in Syracuse, just minutes from three highways: I-81, I-90, and the New York State Thruway. It's even closer to Destiny USA, a six-story mall that has more or less anything you could need, including plenty of chain restaurants.

What's in a Name?

For a decade—from 1997, when NBT Bank Stadium opened, through 2006—Syracuse went by the nickname of "SkyChiefs." It didn't catch on, though, and after years of townspeople largely sticking with just "Chiefs," the team formally reverted for 2007. The club molded its brand around a train theme, as opposed to Native American symbols/culture, as the "Chiefs" moniker might suggest.

The city of Syracuse, probably known best for its awful winters and Syracuse University's Division 1 athletics, is generally mild in the summer.

Attendance isn't great at Chiefs' games, but one team employee characterized Syracuse as an event town. If you can make a game feel like more than just a regular baseball game, one of seventy-or-so throughout the year, people will show up. The Chiefs have worked in recent years to give NBT Bank Stadium that vibe, what with a Walking Dead Night and Country Music Night and a much-hyped Fourth of July fireworks show.

It's a safe bet the stadium will be a bit busier when the Scranton/Wilkes-Barre RailRiders, the Yankees' Triple-A affiliate, visit. Syracuse is known as a Yankees-dominant town. The Pawtucket Red Sox tend to draw a crowd, too.

Quick Bites

Ballpark food not doing it for you? The Chiefs don't stray too much from your standard fare. Here are some nearby options for all times of day:

- **Second North Deli: Nothing fancy, just a quality deli, which is never a bad option**
- **Stella's Diner: Large portions, plus a fascination with Betty Boop**
- **Change of Pace: A bar partly owned by former big league pitcher Steve Grilli, the Chiefs' color analyst for televised games and the father of major leaguer Jason Grilli**
- **Tully's: An upstate New York chain known for its chicken tenders**

Diamond Dig

The Chiefs' recent refocus on promotions and in-game experience resulted in quite the scene one night in June 2016: One hundred women—armed only with small wooden forks—wandering about on their hands and knees, digging up the infield dirt for three worthless tokens that represented so much more.

The team called it a "Diamond Dig." Groundskeeper John Stewart buried three tokens in the infield before the game. One of these tokens was worth a half-carat diamond ring valued at about $900. After the Chiefs' loss to the Louisville Bats, the ladies had free reign. They had thirty minutes to do their digging. It only took twelve for the tokens to be found.

Like a Dream

From the "You never know what you'll see at the ballpark" files: On Father's Day 2015, the Chiefs brought actor Dwier Brown, who played Kevin Costner's character's father in *Field of Dreams*, to NBT Bank Stadium. That afternoon, the Chiefs won on a walk-off hit from Tony Gwynn Jr., who was playing on his first Father's Day without his own dad, Hall of Famer Tony Gwynn, who had died a year prior.

Syracuse has found success with other promotions. Its $1 Thursdays—with hot dogs and soda costing a buck each, most beers only $2—are popular. Between-inning breaks are filled with mascot races (which usually devolve into the participants whomping on each other) and a Human Bobblehead game. Smorol calls them "eighteen opportunities to put on a Broadway show in 180 seconds." They once gave away a bobblehead of Nationals star Bryce Harper dressed as a firefighter. And kids usually run the bases postgame on Sundays.

Past Greats

Here's a partial look at some noteworthy big leaguers who played at NBT Bank Stadium before moving on to The Show.

1990s:

Casey Blake, Chris Carpenter, Kelvim Escobar, Roy Halladay

2000s:

Kevin Cash, Ian Desmond, Marco Estrada, Orlando Hudson, Cesar Izturis, Brandon League, Adam Lind, Alex Rios, Vernon Wells, Jayson Werth, Jordan Zimmermann

2010s:

Danny Espinosa, Lucas Giolito, Bryce Harper, Sandy Leon, Wilson Ramos, Anthony Rendon, Tanner Roark, Stephen Strasburg, Trea Turner

Another name worth mentioning: NFL star Deion Sanders played his final professional baseball games as a member of the Chiefs in 2001.

PNC FIELD

HOME OF THE
Scranton/Wilkes-Barre RailRiders

LOCATION: Moosic, PA

TIME FROM:

BINGHAMTON, NY: 1 hour, 15 minutes

ALLENTOWN, PA: 1 hour, 15 minutes

PHILADELPHIA, PA: 2 hours

NEW YORK, NY: 2 hours, 15 minutes

TRENTON, NJ: 2 hours, 15 minutes

ALBANY, NY: 3 hours

HARTFORD, CT: 3 hours, 15 minutes

OPENED: 1989 (renovated in 2012)

CAPACITY: 10,000

TENANT: Scranton/Wilkes-Barre RailRiders, Triple-A International League (1989–2011, 2013–present)

DISTANCE FROM HOME PLATE: 326 feet to left field, 408 to center, 330 to right

RADIO: 100.7 FM (Wilkes-Barre) and affiliates

Construction Junction

How do you take the notoriously difficult baseball season—already a grind with the travel, long hours and near-daily games—and make it even more so? Make it a season-long road trip.

That was the case for the RailRiders (then called the Scranton/Wilkes-Barre Yankees in 2012 when PNC Field underwent massive in-season renovations that forced them out of their home park for the entire season. While making a temporary name change to Empire State Yankees, so as to try to endear themselves to the entire state of New York, they played "home games" in Rochester, Batavia, Syracuse, Buffalo, Allentown, and Pawtucket.

It was, in a word, awful.

"We knew what we were getting into, knowing we were going to pull this renovation off while playing a full season," said former General Manager Jeremy Ruby, a SWB-area native. "It was a little more to handle than we thought."

Most of the team's home games were in Rochester, about three and a half hours northwest. Scranton/Wilkes-Barre typically sent a full-time staff member or two to help out with logistics. It was far from ideal, but there was a sense among the SWB folks—as well as other International League teams and leaders—that the one-year inconvenience would ultimately be worth it, beneficial for everybody in the long-term.

And, boy, was it ever. PNC Field, once a relic of the 1980s when some minor league ballparks were modeled after the no-longer-standing Veterans Stadium in Philadelphia, now features all of the amenities of modern facilities. Construction crews rebuilt everything except the playing surface and home clubhouse, both of which had been replaced when the club became a Yankees affiliate a few years prior.

The old, dark, and dingy concourse gave way to an open, 360-degree one. "That's a big, big improvement and something that our fans have told us they love," said COO Josh Olerud. Grassy berms and suite levels—previously non-existent—are now popular sections of the park. Regular seats come with cup holders and are angled toward home plate. The new LED video board is nice, too. In the years since the "new" ballpark opened, attendance has been up about one-third over the old ballpark, with more than 400,000 fans visiting PNC Field per year.

As for 2012's Empire State Yankees? They finished 84–60 and made the playoffs. Not bad for a bunch of professional ballplayers/vagabonds.

What's in a Name?

Since the franchise moved to Moosic and PNC Field, its official name has gone through several stages. From 1989 through 2006, when the team was a Philadelphia Phillies affiliate, they were the Scranton/Wilkes-Barre Red Barons. From 2007 through 2011, the team linked up with the New York Yankees and were known as the Scranton/Wilkes-Barre Yankees. For their season-long road trip in 2012 they assumed the moniker of Empire State Yankees. Since 2013, however, they've kept their Scranton/Wilkes-Barre RailRiders name, after the team decided to rebrand in advance of the opening of its renovated ballpark.

You'll notice that those names include "Scranton/Wilkes-Barre," despite the team not being located in either of those towns—Scranton just northeast, Wilkes-Barres a tad southwest. That's an attempt to portray a more regional identity. That five-syllable geographical identifier—Scranton/Wilkes-Barre—is a mouthful, and team executives are well aware of that. They try to shorten it to SWB whenever possible.

The club's name/logo/mascot branding is a mishmash of popular options from a name-the-team contest in 2012. RailRiders, a nod to Scranton's claim as the originator of the electric streetcar, garnered the most votes, but Porcupines was another popular option. The team found middle ground by making their logo a porcupine—a common animal in Northeast Pennsylvania—straddling a rail. One of the mascots, Quill, is a porcupine dressed up as a train conductor.

Hop a Ride

Want to really get that SWB experience? The Electric City Trolley Museum Association runs a trolley from Steamtown Platform in downtown Scranton to PNC Field for select home games.

A Dinger to Remember

The New York Yankees' second half of 2016 deviated from the club's historical norm: trading away veteran players and calling up young ones from Scranton/Wilkes-Barre.

Among them were outfielder Aaron Judge and first baseman Tyler Austin. A few Rail-Riders staffers ventured to Yankee Stadium for a group outing one day in August, and it happened to be both of those players' major

league debuts. In the second inning, in back-to-back plate appearances, both players hit home runs in their first major league at-bats, the first teammates ever to accomplish that feat.

Said one SWB visitor: "We were losing our minds."

Past Greats

Here's a partial look at some noteworthy big leaguers who played at PNC Field before moving on to major league success.

1990s:
Ruben Amaro, Marlon Anderson, Andy Ashby, Mike Lieberthal, Scott Rolen, Jimmy Rollins, Randy Wolf

2000s:
Michael Bourn, Pat Burrell, Marlon Byrd, Melky Cabrera, Francisco Cervelli, Joba Chamberlain, Tyler Clippard, Brett Gardner, Cole Hamels, J.A. Happ, Ryan Howard, Phil Hughes, Austin Jackson, Mark Melancon, Brett Myers, Chase Utley, Shane Victorino, Chien-Ming Wang

2010s:
Dellin Betances, Aaron Judge, Ivan Nova, Gary Sanchez

Have a Seat

Among the benefits of the 2012 renovations is that PNC Field is full of great places to sit. Gone is the gigantic, mostly empty upper deck. Here to stay is a walkable outfield and luxury suites.

One tier of field-level seats constitutes the main bowl. Seats from dugout end to dugout end are a bit more expensive than seats from dugout end to foul pole. The upper level includes a row of eighteen suites plus two party decks—one on either end—in the Mohegan Sun Club & Suite Level.

The right-field corner includes a set of bleachers next to the Budweiser RailHouse, a bar area with high-top counters. Across the way in the left-field corner is a party pavilion for large groups. In between are two berm areas—with trees growing right out of the hillside—and other standing-room-only sections.

Parking is aplenty at PNC Field. Three on-site lots are usually enough, but on the occasions the RailRiders draw especially large crowds—holidays, nice weekends—there are private lots nearby to supplement what the team can offer.

The entire setup is built near the foot of Montage Mountain, a popular skiing spot come wintertime. Most of the non-baseball entertainment is at the Shoppes at Montage, a large mall just beyond the outfield fence with a movie theatre, a handful of chain restaurants, and three different Marriotts. If you want something more taste-of-the-town, try Nonno's, an Italian place within that shopping center.

Willing to take a bit of a drive? Neighboring Old Forge is the so-called Pizza Capital of the World, and Revello's is said to be the best. Old Forge–style pizza comes in two types: red (doughy crust, a ton of cheese) and white (cheese between two crusts, yielding a calzone-ish product). The rectangular pies are called "trays," and slices are called "cuts." Don't mess it up!

PNC Field is Lit

In SWB, where major league fandom is split roughly in half between Yankees supporters and Phillies fans, one of the RailRiders' most successful promotions involved winning over the former, who tend to be rather traditional. Every Friday home game, which were capped by a fireworks show, RailRiders players wore all black and neon colors—a dramatic departure from the usual blue and white—and the team sold similarly styled merchandise in the team store. The catch? It glowed in the dark. When the stadium lights dimmed for the postgame fireworks, anyone wearing the merchandise lit up. By season's end, nearly everyone in attendance participated in Glow-in-the-Park Fridays.

The RailRiders take advantage, too, of being affiliated with the Yankees, as one might expect of a club partnered with arguably the most recognized and popular sports brand in the world. Joe DiMaggio and Mariano Rivera were among the New York greats honored with giveaways in 2016.

Ballpark Eats

The best part of getting food at PNC Field is you don't have to miss the game while you wait in line, thanks to the open concourse. The second-best part is the RailRiders get some big league help with their food, outsourcing that responsibility to Legends Hospitality, the same company the New York Yankees use. Among your item options:

- Revello's pizza, the most popular item, from a popular pizza joint in nearby Old Forge
- Walking tacos, essentially a taco salad in a bag
- Mixed drinks poured into freshly cut pineapples
- Supreme Nacho stand, with momma-, daddy-, and baby-sized portions
- Pulled pork, beef brisket, and other BBQ

COCA-COLA PARK

HOME OF THE
Lehigh Valley IronPigs

LOCATION: Allentown, PA

TIME FROM:

READING, PA:	45 minutes
PHILADELPHIA, PA:	1 hour, 15 minutes
SCRANTON, PA:	1 hour, 15 minutes
NEW YORK, NY:	1 hour, 30 minutes
BALTIMORE, MD:	2 hours, 30 minutes
HARTFORD, CT:	3 hours, 15 minutes

OPENED: 2008

CAPACITY: 10,100

TENANT: Lehigh Valley IronPigs, Triple-A International League (2008–present)

DISTANCE FROM HOME PLATE: 323 feet to left field, 400 to center, 325 to right

RADIO: 1230 AM (Easton) and 1320 AM (Allentown)

New and Nice

Coca-Cola Park is, simply put, a top-notch minor league ballpark and experience. The IronPigs regularly rank at or near the top of per-game attendance lists and various best-of rankings. The promotions are creative and in-game entertainment nonstop. They work in community goings-on, from Musikfest to the local Miracle League, and every home game is broadcast in HD on local TV with a twelve-camera setup. So in Lehigh Valley—or just "the Valley" if you live there—the baseball culture is a good one (as you might hope after a $50 million stadium gets built).

It helps, of course, that the region has an industrial background that lends itself to a goofy team name. The Lehigh Valley, the third-largest metropolitan area in Pennsylvania, was known for its steelmaking, particularly Bethlehem Steel. Pig irons are crude blocks of steel produced at mills in the Valley and mostly shipped off to Pittsburgh.

Video Game Whiz

The IronPigs drew praise—and some weird looks—when they installed a Urinal Game System into their men's bathrooms in the spring of 2013, the first North American sporting venue to do so. The pee-controlled mini-games are activated by a man's presence, and he plays by aiming his stream. At game's/pee's end, the game displays a code that he can enter online to see how he stacks up against other restroom-goers.

When owners Joseph Finley and Craig Stein—successful MLB businessmen who know what moves the needle—bought the Triple-A Ottawa franchise around 2006 and moved it to Allentown, a name-the-team contest yielded one entry they particularly loved: IronPigs. The name of the fan who submitted that nickname? Ron Steele. True story.

IronPigs won the contest, and the branding opportunities came easy. FeRROUS and FeFe—both a play on "Fe" being the symbol for the chemical element of iron—are two of the team's mascots. The logo is quite literally a ferocious pig made out of steel. And, years after the IronPigs' birth, the pig theme paved the way for a popular bacon-based marketing campaign (but more on that later).

Pick a Seat

The thing about going to a game at Coca-Cola Park is that there are a lot—a lot—of options on where to sit. It starts with the main bowl, which is relatively straightforward: twenty sections of field-level seats stretching from the right-field foul pole to shallow left field. The abnormal part: four thirty-person suites at field level between the home and away dugouts, an increasingly popular feature in some of the newer minor league parks.

A small second deck includes club-level seats and a row of suites. At either end of the club level is the Party Porch, which includes group sections for thirty to sixty-five people and comes with buffet access.

Also in foul territory, you have your usual kids' zone and a picnic area down the left-field

line. In the right-field corner is what the team calls the TD Bank Plaza, a hangout area next to the ballpark's main entrance.

What sets Coca-Cola Park apart from some other also-nice stadiums with 360-degree concourses is its outfield seating options. In left-center is a berm, a somewhat standard feature, but the setups in left and right fields are far less common. In right, the Bacon Strip is like a poor man's Green Monster—two levels of seating and drink rails on top of a 17-foot wall. In left, you have the Pig Pen, two rows of seating—one set of wide, fixed seats and one set of higher bar stools—with an unusual view: the

game in front of you, the bullpens behind you. Behind that, the Tiki Terrace & Oasis, a balcony that overlooks the field.

International League, Sort Of

When the Ottawa Lynx ended their nearly quarter-century tenure at Ottawa Baseball Stadium and moved to Allentown after the 2007 season, the Triple-A "International" League officially had no more teams in Canada. The Buffalo Bisons are closest.

The IronPigs are a hot ticket in the area—even with average attendance dipping into the still-impressive 8,000s in recent years—and the team has the parking to match. There are six lots around the stadium, all of them fittingly named after Coke products.

One reason for so much parking is the neighborhood's industrial park vibe, usually a good thing for minor league baseball because it means lots of space and quiet surroundings come game time.

The whole setup is set aside from downtown Allentown, which isn't exactly a destination but has seen some recent revival. The PPL Center, a sports arena that opened in 2014, has helped with that. It's home of the Lehigh Valley Phantoms of the American Hockey League, which is like the Triple-A equivalent in hockey. The Phantoms are to the NHL's Philadelphia Flyers what the IronPigs are to MLB's Philadelphia Phillies.

Bacon, USA

In the business of minor league baseball, where gimmicks and gags are more important than games, doing weird, offbeat stuff is almost a necessity for long-term success. And the IronPigs crush the weird, offbeat game.

Past Greats

Here's a partial look at some of those who played at Coca-Cola Park on the way to the big leagues. It's not a long list, but so it goes when a park is only a few years old (and associated with a parent team, the Phillies, that has seen little success in most of those years).

2000s:
Antonio Bastardo, J.A. Happ

2010s:
Maikel Franco, Freddy Galvis, Ken Giles, Ryne Sandberg (manager)

Unlike Double-A Reading, which has sent players toward Philadelphia for more than a half-century (in recent years with stops in Lehigh Valley in between), the IronPigs have only been around for a decade. A list of successful alums can only grow with time.

So You Want to Get an Autograph?

Part of the appeal of going to a minor league game is the possibility of obtaining players' signatures. The idea that this professional ballplayer holding your baseball and your pen might one day be a major league star? That's pretty cool. Here are some tips on how to go about it.

DOS

- Know the rules. Some teams designate certain times and areas—next to the dugouts one hour before the game, for example—or have an "Autograph Alley" table on the concourse where a chosen player will sign.

- Know faces. It's pretty awkward if you shout one player's name, trying to get his attention, only to learn you have the wrong guy. Most prospects' headshots are online, so make sure to take a look beforehand.

- Have patience. The best times to get autographs are during batting practice or when players are leaving the ballpark. That means showing up early and staying late.

- Be prepared. Make sure you have the right tools. If you want a player to sign a baseball, have a well-functioning pen. If you want a player to sign a photo or baseball card, a Sharpie is better.

DONT'S

- Try too hard. If it's getting close to game time, your window is probably closed. Players tend to lock in in that last half-hour or more.

- Be old. Let's be honest, it's a little weird when grown men are loitering, trying to get much younger men to put pen to paper.

- Be rude. This is a good rule of thumb for life generally, but especially when you're asking a stranger to give you something for free.

That includes what almost certainly ranks among the most successful marketing campaigns in the history of the minor leagues: Turning Lehigh Valley into Bacon, USA.

It began in 2014, when after several years of "Iron" and "Pig" jokes, the IronPigs tried to answer a fundamental minor league question:

How could they breathe some life and energy into their merchandise sales? The answer? Bacon, bacon, and more bacon.

That February, the team unveiled its new Saturday home uniforms: a cap with a bacon-strip logo, jerseys with "Pig" underlined in bacon, and pants with bacon piping down

the legs. The campaign was an immediate hit. Within seventy-two hours, the IronPigs sold bacon-logo hats to all fifty states. The scratch-and-sniff bacon t-shirts were popular, too.

The IronPigs decided to, if you will, ham it up. They added bacon items to the concession stands. Hambone, a lovable loser, became the most popular mascot. The team hosted a Bacon 5K Challenge, which included a half-pound bacon-eating challenge at the halfway point and a piece of chocolate-covered bacon at race's end to celebrate. It also built the Bacon Strip seating in right field.

The team has since given Lehigh Valley the "Bacon, USA," nickname. In 2016, their Saturday jerseys featured that sprawled across the front instead of "Lehigh Valley" or "IronPigs."

The bacon obsession gave birth to another meat-based spinoff in 2016: the Lehigh Valley Cheesesteaks. The IronPigs changed their name for one night in June for Salute to Phil-adelphia Night, with the iconic Philly delicacy serving as the pillar. The players' jerseys had "Steaks" written across the chest in "Cheese Wiz" yellow, and a fan vote resulted in hats featuring cheesesteaks "wit" onions (as opposed to "witout").

Is anybody else hungry?

DOUBLE-A
BALLPARKS

HADLOCK FIELD

HOME OF THE
Portland Sea Dogs

LOCATION: Portland, ME

TIME FROM:

AUGUSTA, ME: 1 hour

MANCHESTER, NH: 1 hour, 30 minutes

BOSTON, MA: 1 hour, 45 minutes

WORCESTER, MA: 2 hours, 15 minutes

HARTFORD, CT: 3 hours

NEW YORK, NY: 5 hours

OPENED: 1994

CAPACITY: 7,368

TENANT: Portland Sea Dogs, Double-A Eastern League (1994–present)

PAST TENANTS: None

DISTANCE FROM HOME PLATE: 315 feet to left field, 400 to center, 330 to right

RADIO: 95.5 and 95.9 FM (Portland)

A Regional Attraction

Hadlock Field is much older than the Portland Sea Dogs, long the home of the Portland High School Bulldogs and Deering High School Rams. It is named after Edson Hadlock Jr., the baseball coach at Portland High from 1950 to 1978. When the pro team came to town in the early 1990s, the city built the stadium around the long-existent field to meet the Double-A team's needs. The high school teams continue to share the space in the spring.

The Sea Dogs came to be because Major League Baseball added two teams, the Florida Marlins and Colorado Rockies, for the 1993 season, so Minor League Baseball needed more teams to match. Portland wound up affiliated with the Marlins, a relationship that lasted nine seasons before the Sea Dogs linked up with the Red Sox, a much more logical geographical fit.

Hot Start in the Cold

People in New England like baseball. It's true in Boston, and Mainers proved it to be true in Portland almost immediately. In February 1994, a month and a half before the Sea Dogs' first game, fans waited in line overnight in 12°F weather to buy tickets. The home opener sold out in hours. That season, the Sea Dogs filled Hadlock to capacity for more than two-thirds of their home dates. By mid-1996, they welcomed their 1 millionth fan. In 2016, they hit 9 million.

The Sea Dogs–Red Sox affiliation "took a good thing and made it better," as Chris Cameron, Portland vice president, put it. Attendance had always been good, but in 2003—the first year of the new partnership—the Sea Dogs saw about 500 additional fans per game. Portland is in the heart of Red Sox Nation, and over the years the Sea Dogs have adapted their ballpark and brand to fit in as the Red Sox's little brother—much like the Triple-A Pawtucket Red Sox in Pawtucket, Rhode Island. It's not uncommon to see Sea Dogs merchandise in all corners of New England (and even beyond).

Despite a lengthy list of notable MLB alums, the Sea Dogs haven't fared especially well on the field through the years. Only one of their six division titles resulted in an Eastern League championship. That came in 2006, when future big leaguers Jacoby Ellsbury and Brandon Moss led the way offensively.

New England Charm

The Sea Dogs, in their twenty-plus-year history, have had the pleasant problem of not having enough room for all the people who want to attend games. That has led to periodic expansion projects—four in all—bringing Hadlock Field up to 7,368 seats.

Many of the non-original seats, including a group area down the left-field line and a handful of box-seat sections beyond first base, feel wedged in and haphazardly placed. The result is a disjointed feel as you walk about the park, but in a curiously charming way. Consider it part of Hadlock's New England charm.

The odd setup is in part because Hadlock Field is landlocked, built in the early '90s

into a much older neighborhood. Park Avenue prevents the Sea Dogs from expanding in foul territory, and the combination of Fitzpatrick Stadium in right field and a railroad track/I-295 in left field limits how far they can build out in the outfield.

The neighborhood, though, does have its benefits. Hadlock is part of the Portland Sports Complex, which includes Fitzpatrick (a high school football stadium), William B. Troubh Ice Arena, and the Portland Exposition Building. That last one, the second longest continuously used exposition center in the United States, is home to the Maine Red Claws of the NBA Developmental League and the Sea Dogs' visitors' locker room.

The resulting parking situation can be tricky. There are lots of options, but not all of them

are obvious, so the Sea Dogs try to help with signage around the neighborhood. There is a parking garage across the street, plus the Fitzpatrick Stadium lot in the outfield. Other local businesses usually sell their spots, too.

Weekend Getaway

The city of Portland, of course, largely speaks for itself. A popular vacation spot, Portland has beaches (lovely), eateries (ranging from well-known to hidden), museums, and shopping. There's enough to do that you can easily fill a long weekend with a Sea Dogs game and other attractions.

In Hadlock Field's main seating bowl, stretching from shallow left field to about first base, there are three levels: box seats (closest to the field), reserved seats (above a walkway), and general-admission bleachers. The Coco-Cola Picnic Area down the right-field line can accommodate large groups. The only outfield seating—the only place you can catch a fair ball—is the U.S. Cellular Pavilion in right field. Built in advance of the 2006 season, the pavilion offers several rows of seats and counters/ledges, not unlike the Green Monster in Boston. It also neighbors the elevated Sea Dogs bullpen. During quiet moments as a reliever warms, you can hear the pop of the catcher's mitt.

Past Greats

Here's a partial look at some noteworthy big leaguers who made stops in Portland before their major league successes.

1990s:

Ryan Dempster, Kevin Millar, Brad Penny, Edgar Renteria, Gary Sheffield

2000s:

Daniel Bard, Josh Beckett, Clay Buchholz, Jacoby Ellsbury, Adrian Gonzalez, Jon Lester, Jed Lowrie, Jonathan Papelbon, Hanley Ramirez, Josh Reddick, Anibal Sanchez, Kevin Youkilis

2010s:

Matt Barnes, Mookie Betts, Xander Bogaerts, Jackie Bradley Jr., Jose Iglesias, Blake Swihart

Sticking with the Sox

As one might expect, given the Sea Dogs' affiliation and geographical proximity to Boston, the team has worked in recent years to mimic the Fenway experience and tap into that base as much as possible. That filters right down to the outfield signage, which includes a number of New England mainstays: Hood, W.B. Mason, and Sullivan Tire. The last of those urges players to "hit it here," through a tiny hole above the

of Maine, but do draw from northern Massachusetts—especially when a top-notch prospect is suiting up, drawing more hardcore Red Sox fans eager to catch a glimpse of the Next Big Thing.

Even when there aren't any noteworthy names in the lineup, the Sea Dogs incorporate their Red Sox connections as part of the day-to-day in-game experience. A small scoreboard displays the status of that day's Red Sox game, and on the sharp video board in right field—new in 2014—the Sea Dogs occasionally show highlights from Boston's most recent game.

If you venture to Hadlock and/or Portland, be sure to try a Sea Dog biscuit, a dessert as old as the Sea Dogs made by the Sanford-based Shain's of Maine Ice Cream. It's vanilla ice cream sandwiched between two chocolate-chip cookies. "I know it sounds fairly basic, but there's something about a Sea Dog Biscuit that will hook you," Cameron said. "It has an iconic status throughout the state of Maine. People are infatuated with it."

The Maine Monster

Even if you've never visited, you would probably recognize Hadlock Field's best-known feature: a wall 37 feet high, worn by the weather, and unmistakably green.

The Maine Monster, the Sea Dogs' likeness of Fenway Park's Green Monster, went up over the course of several months after the 2002 season when the team made the natural move of working with the Red Sox, putting another Boston farm team in New England. The Sea Dogs wanted to embrace its new parent team's history and tradition, and the Maine Monster was the physical centerpiece of that effort.

right-field wall. And if they do? The player and a fan win $10,000. (It's been done once, by Sean Coyle in 2014.)

In sticking with the Maine/New England theme, the Sea Dogs even used to have their own Citgo Sign, like the iconic Boston landmark, but that sponsorship ended. A pair of gigantic inflatable L.L. Bean boots, another Maine icon, hangs out in right field. When the Sea Dogs hit a home run or finish off a win, a lighthouse pops out and lights up in center field.

When Hadlock is packed, it's full of Red Sox fans. The Sea Dogs market throughout the state

Dean Sciaraffa helped it happen. A lifelong Portland-area resident, Sciaraffa owned H.B. Fleming, a local pile-driving company. The Sea Dogs called him that fall with a request: They needed his people to drive some pile—steel poles—not far from the Hadlock property line in left field. Winter was coming, and they were in a hurry. "It all came about quickly," Sciaraffa said.

Before Halloween, Sciaraffa & Co. drilled a series of deep holes (three feet in diameter) where the wall would soon stand. Then they drove sixty-foot poles about twenty-three feet into the ground—leaving thirty-seven feet of pole above ground—and filled in the holes with concrete to stabilize the poles. Over the course of about two weeks, H.B. Fleming erected the Maine Monster's steel skeleton. The Sea Dogs hired a local carpenter to put on the "skin," the forward-facing two- by six-foot, pressure-treated wooden planks that constitute the actual wall. The entire project was all but done by the New Year.

The Maine Monster isn't an exact replica of its Boston counterpart—it's made of wood instead of metal, and it doesn't stretch quite as far into center field—and does require regular maintenance. It gets a fresh coat of paint every year, and the Sea Dogs check on the wooden planks twice annually. More than a decade later, some of the originals remain.

The details add to the Monsters' resemblance. In Maine, the wall has a scoreboard (albeit electronic instead of manual) and used to be adorned with a Citgo Sign and Coke bottle a la Boston. And just as Fenway has the initials of former owners Tom and Jean Yawkey written in Morse code on the Green Monster, Maine has the initials of Dan and Harriet Burke, the Sea

Dogs' founders. It's a subtle nod to the history of both teams.

The Maine Monster is more than just an aesthetic, however. It's practical. Much like Fenway, a purported 310 feet down the left-field line, Hadlock is just 315. For a long time, that resulted in a hitters' paradise of sorts. Adding a 37-foot obstruction helped level the field of play.

There is a value to the players development-wise, too. The Green Monster is unlike anything in the major leagues, and it has a reputation as being difficult to learn and near-impossible for visitors to defend. The Red Sox start to get their minor leaguers acclimated to that sort of scenario with Green Monster-esque walls in Portland and Low-A Greenville, plus one at their spring training home, JetBlue Park in Fort Myers, Florida.

Take Andrew Benintendi, the Red Sox's first-round pick in the 2015 MLB draft, as an example. A center fielder by trade, Benintendi was knocking down the door for a major league promotion in 2016 but had little chance of breaking through at center because the Red Sox were well stocked at that position. So, after Benintendi spent some time with the Sea Dogs, the club tried him in left field, with the Maine Monster over his shoulder.

"It gives you [a] sense of what you're going to be dealing with at Fenway Park," says Cameron. "And some players, they're never going to make it to Boston. This is their opportunity. It's such an iconic thing. Even though it's on a smaller scale, it's a pretty cool thing to play with."

There are offensive and defensive benefits. Young hitters can learn to either pull the ball off the Monster or hit it the other way—depending on their handedness—for an easy double. And while it's impossible to replicate the odd bounces batted balls take off the Green Monster after decades of dents, there is something to be gained from dealing with the mere phys-

ical presence. How deep should you play? How shallow? How hard do you need to throw a frozen rope to second base? Is that would-be homer going to turn into a single?

"When you get to Fenway Park and you're standing in left field with that 37-foot wall behind you, it can be intimidating," Sea Dogs GM Geoff Iacuessa said. "To be able to be out here and play balls off that wall in a game situation—and also to be able to do it during batting practice—there's a value to it."

A handful of times per season, Sciaraffa—the pile-driver boss—visits Hadlock for a game. He brought his kids all the time when they were young, and they liked catching a glimpse of prospects before they made headlines in Boston. In 2016, one of those prospects was Benintendi, playing in front of the wall Sciaraffa helped build.

"Every so often," Sciaraffa said, "you think back and think you were part of that job."

Ballpark Eats

The Sea Dogs' concessions go a step beyond typical ballpark food, especially with the Shipyard Grill down the left-base line, which offers sandwiches, wraps, and salads in an attempt to be a wee bit healthy. If you want to be unhealthy, though, get to know the Mount Dessert Island. The $20 monstrosity includes: a fried dough shell, soft-serve ice cream, hot fudge, caramel, whipped cream, rainbow sprinkles, Reese's Pieces, M&Ms, and cherries. And it's served in a full-size Sea Dogs batting helmet. "It'll feed you," Cameron says, "and five others."

NORTHEAST DELTA DENTAL STADIUM

HOME OF THE

New Hampshire Fisher Cats

LOCATION:	Manchester, NH
TIME FROM:	
BOSTON, MA:	1 hour
PORTLAND, ME:	1 hour, 30 minutes
PROVIDENCE, RI:	1 hour, 45 minutes
HARTFORD, CT:	2 hours
ALBANY, NY:	3 hours, 15 minutes
NEW YORK, NY:	4 hours
OPENED:	2005
CAPACITY:	6,500
TENANT:	New Hampshire Fisher Cats, Double-A Eastern League (2005–present)
DISTANCE FROM HOME PLATE:	326 feet to left field, 400 to center, 306 to right
RADIO:	610 AM (Manchester)

New Digs

Ask some of the early New Hampshire Fisher Cats what they remember about playing in Manchester, and they respond with a key question: The old park or the new one?

The Fisher Cats played their first season, 2004, at Gill Stadium, a small park about a century old that has been host to mostly amateur baseball through the years. The arrangement was temporary. A mile and a half away, on the banks of the Merrimack River, crews were at work on what is now known as Northeast Delta Dental Stadium—originally Fisher Cats Ballpark—which opened in 2005.

Northeast Delta, appropriately located at 1 Line Drive, and the Fisher Cats have since become community pillars, winning numerous local honors: "Best Sporting Event to Take Clients

Family Business

Arguably the most popular living creature at Northeast Delta, Ollie the golden retriever, retired after 2016, ending his six-year career as the Fisher Cats' bat dog. In what amounted to an act of professional fetch, Ollie used to grab New Hampshire players' bats at the end of their plate appearances for part of every home game.

Ollie had followed in the footsteps of his father, Chase, the original bat dog for the Trenton Thunder. Ollie's brother, Derby, still serves in that role for the Thunder alongside Ollie's nephew, Rookie.

To" by the Best of Business Awards, the "Best New Hampshire Sports Team" by *New Hampshire Magazine*, and "Favorite Sporting Event for Families" by *Parenting New Hampshire Magazine*.

All that love stands in drastic historical comparison to some initial reactions to the club's presence. Before the Fisher Cats were the Fisher Cats, they were the New Hampshire Primaries, a management-selected name that was meant to pay homage to the state's "First in the Nation" primary during the presidential election cycle every four years. The logo featured an elephant and a donkey holding baseball bats.

Public outcry was immediate and immense. Three days after the November 2003 announcement, the *New Hampshire Union Leader*—the state's leading newspaper—ran a front-page article about an online petition started by two local fans who asked the team to reconsider. Four days after that, the team indeed reconsidered, starting a name-the-team contest that resulted in Fisher Cats edging out Manchester Millers, Granite State Mountain Men, and New Hampshire Granite. New Hampshire Primaries was a distant fifth in the final voting.

And so the Fisher Cats were born. A year later, the ballpark. It took a couple of years to catch on, but by the end of the 2000s, Fisher Cat games were a hit, the team drawing well over 5,000 fans per night.

Attendance has declined—a relative phrase, to be sure—in recent years, coincidentally in contrast with the success of the Toronto Blue Jays, New Hampshire's parent team, and the stream of quality prospects coming through. The Fisher Cats averaged 4,834 fans per game in 2016, their lowest mark in a decade.

As for the New Hampshire Primaries, well, the team that never was once in a while gets on the field. The Fisher Cats have broken out those unis for pseudo-throwback nights on occasion.

Have a Seat

Northeast Delta Dental Stadium faces away from the Merrimack River, so there is no water view. There is, however, a great view of the game no matter where you sit, the beauty of the open concourse design.

The Fisher Cats differ from most teams in that they offer a single pricing option on individual tickets, any seat in the main bowl costing the same amount—in 2016 it was $14 on game day, $12 in advance—whether you're sitting in Section 100 in the left-field corner or Section

Ballpark Eats

The Fisher Cats' new signature concession item in 2016 was The Squealer—bacon, ham, sausage, pepperoni, pulled pork, cheddar cheese, and barbecue sauce, all on a bun shaped like a pig face. Alas, it turned out to be a 2016-only specialty, but that's the sort of creativity (and cholesterol-raising) stuff you can expect at Northeast Delta.

If wildly unhealthy isn't your thing, that's okay. The Fisher Cats are into healthy, too, and have one stand, The Healthy Plate, dedicated to it. The soups, salads, and smoothies tend to be popular.

Make sure to wash it all down with some fried Oreos.

What's in a Name?

A fisher cat—or, if you listen to animal experts who critique the team's name, just a "fisher"—is a relative of the weasel found in the northeastern United States and Canada. Or, as one longtime Manchester-area resident and Fisher Cats observer put it: "They're basically just a mean mountain predator situation."

Fisher cats are ferocious, but more often heard than seen. They make an awful, high-pitched screaming sound. If you run into a fisher, better to turn around.

109 behind home plate. Hanging above the concourse is the suite level, bookended by Party Decks. Those group sections fit 100 people and come with one of the suites.

A big draw is in left field: The Samuel Adams Bar & Grill, a full-service restaurant that opens to those with game tickets two hours before first pitch, making it a prime spot to hang out and grab something to eat while watching batting practice. It's also a go-to in the area for private events—including wedding receptions—year-round.

One of the main features of the neighborhood is plainly visible from anywhere in the ballpark, a Hilton Garden Inn in left-center. It's the default temporary housing for major leaguers visiting New Hampshire for a rehab appearance, and rooms that face the field offer a tremendous view of the field. It has drawn comparisons to the center-field hotel at the Blue Jays' Rogers Centre in Toronto.

Parking isn't as easy as it is in other minor league towns, but you can pick one of two options: a bit of a walk or a bit of a wait. The limited on-site parking usually means a postgame wait, with the one-way-in/one-way-out traffic a result of the neighborhood's configuration (including a river on one side and a railroad on the other). There are also plenty of private lots not too far, if you're down to walk.

Stanton Park and especially Merrimack River Park are within walking distance. The Fisher Cats host a 3K every year along the river, and the city is said to be trying to reenergize the area.

Past Greats

Here's a partial look at some noteworthy big leaguers who have played at Northeast Delta Dental Stadium in its brief history. More than eighty Fisher Cats have reached the majors in all.

2000s:

Brandon League, Adam Lind, Dustin McGowan, Marc Rzepczynski

2010s:

Henderson Alvarez, Travis d'Arnaud, Sam Dyson, Yan Gomes, Adeiny Hechavarria, Kevin Pillar, Aaron Sanchez, Marcus Stroman

Note how there are more significant names in the second group. The Toronto Blue Jays, who have had far more success in the 2010s than 2000s, have been the Fisher Cats' parent team for the entirety of their existence.

The ballpark is set aside from downtown Manchester, which offers some nightlife. A go-to lunch spot for the fine folks who work for the Fisher Cats is Murphy's Taproom, a four-minute drive from the stadium and right next to the all so-popular Murphy's Diner.

Blurred Allegiances

After more than a decade in Manchester, the Fisher Cats have become a local favorite. It's their team in their city, and because it's Double-A baseball a bunch of the players are ticketed for the majors. That's pretty fun.

But Manchester is also in the heart of Red Sox Nation. Locals love their Red Sox, their team and their parents' team and their grandparents' team. Northeast Delta Dental Stadium typically sees a bit of an attendance bump when the Portland Sea Dogs, Boston's Eastern League affiliate, visit. New England baseball fans also have a reputation as being smart ones, with an interest in the prospects—whether they belong to the Red Sox or Blue Jays or any other EL parent team—that come through.

If you're not a hardcore baseball fan and you'd rather be entertained by more than just the on-field goings-on, that's okay too. The makeshift jousting and sumo wrestling competitions highlight the between-inning games. And while the Fisher Cats don't have a whole lot of specialty promotions, they go hard on Star Wars Night—so much so that they raised $5,000 for a local hospital that day in 2016.

DUNKIN' DONUTS PARK

HOME OF THE
Hartford Yard Goats

LOCATION:	Hartford, CT
TIME FROM:	
BOSTON, MA:	1 hour, 30 minutes
PROVIDENCE, RI:	1 hour, 30 minutes
ALBANY, NY:	1 hour, 45 minutes
NEW YORK, NY:	2 hours
MANCHESTER, NH:	2 hours
OPENED:	2017
CAPACITY:	6,056
TENANT:	Hartford Yard Goats, Double-A Eastern League
DISTANCE FROM HOME PLATE:	325 to left field, 400 feet to center, 317 to right
RADIO:	1410 AM (Hartford)

Ugly Breakup

Dunkin' Donuts Park—scheduled to open in 2017, a year later than originally planned—is the lovechild of the Hartford Yard Goats and the City of Hartford, a result of about a year and a half of secret negotiations that brought professional baseball back to Connecticut's capital.

The Yards Goats had spent more than three decades in nearby New Britain, most of that time as the Rock Cats, when they shocked the community with a June 2014 announcement that come 2016, they would move to Hartford and play under a new name. The announcement was a surprise, too, to New Britain Mayor Erin Stewart, who fumed alongside her constituents.

For the team, the lure of a brand-new, souped-up stadium was too much to turn down. The city would foot the $56-million bill to build Dunkin' Donuts Park in the heart of downtown Hartford. The Rock Cats would finish out their lease at New Britain Stadium in 2015 before packing up.

Then, as publicly funded construction projects are wont to do, the stadium ended up behind schedule. The Yard Goats pushed their home opening day back from April to mid-June. Then to July, then to August, then to 2017. The Hartford Yard Goats did not play a single game in Hartford in 2016.

Instead, the team played about a dozen games at Dodd Stadium in Norwich, Connecticut, and a bunch more at Northeast Delta Dental Stadium in Manchester, New Hampshire. Most often, the Yard Goats were the "home" team at their opponents' home ballpark. Hartford averaged 799 fans per home game.

"It wasn't easy," said Yards Goats General Manager Tim Restall.

When the Yard Goats ended their season-long road trip around Labor Day, the future of Dunkin' Donuts Park was in question. Involved parties—team, city, insurance company, contractors—bickered over who was responsible for what. The Yard Goats and the Eastern League at one point threatened to leave Hartford if the situation wasn't resolved. The reported estimated cost of the stadium ballooned to more than $70 million.

In New Britain, meanwhile, professional baseball stayed alive, with the New Britain Bees of the independent Atlantic League calling New Britain Stadium home.

As the temperatures cooled, so did the tempers in Hartford. The Yard Goats began their offseason planning with a hope and an expectation—but not a guarantee—that Dunkin' Donuts Park would open in the spring of 2017.

What's in a Name?

The Yard Goats, perhaps more than any other rebranding minor league team in recent memory, drew national attention for their new name. Most of it was confusion. A who Goat? A Yard what?

A yard goat, it turns it, is an antiquated term for a train that stayed in the rail yard, helping cars from track to track. The baseball team bailed on that history when it came to marketing, though, and understandably so. It's a lot easier to sell a cute goat than it is an old locomotive.

Have a Seat

Dunkin' Donuts Park is designed with gaudy ambitions: To allow fans to visit eight to ten times and have eight to ten different experiences. It helps that the stadium, when it's open, will hands-down be one of the nicest in all of the minor leagues, providing fans with any vantage point they could hope for at a major league stadium, but in smaller quantities.

"The days of sitting for nine innings at a baseball game in a tight seat are over," Restall said.

The concourse is wide, open, and 360 degrees. The main bowl is mostly standard—section after section, from medium-depth left field

Blurred Lines

Connecticut, fandom-wise, has long been a beast difficult to wrangle. Boston or New York? In Hartford, which is about thirty minutes from the Massachusetts state line, leans Boston (or Red Sox, at least), but includes plenty of Yankee diehards. Less so when it comes to the Mets, though. Poor Mets.

Ballpark Eats

When it comes to food and the Yard Goats, know this: Tim Restall, the team's general manager, has a background in food and beverage. It's a safe bet that Dunkin' Donuts Park's concessions will be top-notch. He said he treats the ballpark as "the largest restaurant in Connecticut."

What the menu at that restaurant will look like over the long-term has yet to develop, but Restall is focused on variety—vegetarian and seafood options, for example, in addition to the regular stuff.

One mainstay will be Hartford's Neighborhood Flavors, a kiosk with a rotating cast of local eateries showcasing their foods. It'll be a chance for the mom-and-pop type of restaurants to shine.

to medium-depth right field in foul territory—except for dugout suites on the nearside of each dugout. They fit up to forty people, and the front rows of those spaces are closer to home plate than the pitcher is. In the last rows of most of the regular field-box sections, the Yard Goats installed high-top swivel chairs.

One level up are the luxury suites, plus the 7,000-square foot YG Club behind home plate. On the same level down the right-field line is a party deck and more terrace seating.

What sets Dunkin' Donuts Park apart from its contemporaries is the quality and quantity of outfield seating options.

The two-tier right-field porch gives the park a bit of a major league feel. The Budweiser Sky Bar consumes center. In left and left-center fields, the Picnic Pavilion is Green Monster-esque, with several rows of tall swivel seats and drink rails—similar to the Portland Sea Dogs' setup in right field, though not as high or steep. Next to the left-field foul pole are two sections of grandstands. On the foul side of the foul pole, The Bear BBQ Pit, a ballpark version of the Hartford eatery. The brick-and-mortar restaurant is a five-minute drive away. Who doesn't like barbecue?

The visual extras at Dunkin' Donuts Park are many. The video board in left field is 80 feet wide and 40 feet tall, a state-of-the-art model. On top of the video board is a 15-foot-tall coffee cup that will spout steam every time the Yard Goats hit a home run. And right field has 240 feet of LED ribbon board.

Parking will be interesting, with Hartford being a city and all. The lots in the neighborhood—mostly off Main Street, Trumbull Street, and Market Street—are privately operated, so the Yard Goats will point fans toward them as opposed to collecting money themselves.

Hanging Around

Here's the thing about hanging around Dunkin' Donuts Park's neighborhood: You probably won't want to for too long.

The hope in putting the stadium right on Main Street, visible from the minutes-away I-84, was that it would breathe some life into a neighborhood that has long needed it, stretching the bustling downtown area to the other side of the highway. Whether that happens, we'll see. For now, fair warning.

That area of Hartford does have something to offer, though. The area around the ballpark is said to be developing. The XL Center, home to the AHL's Hartford Wolf Pack and UConn men's basketball and hockey, and the plenty of eateries that surround it are six minutes by foot from Dunkin' Donuts Park. There are also a couple of hotels in the immediate vicinity. Not

Past Greats

Since 2016 was the Yard Goats' first season, and since nobody has played at Dunkin' Donuts Park entering 2017, here is a look at some of the franchise's noteworthy alumni when it was the New Britain Rock Cats (1997 through 2015)—just to give you an idea of the sort of legacy a team can build over time. The Rock Cats were a Twins affiliate for every season but their last, when they linked up with the Rockies.

1990s:
Torii Hunter, Jacque Jones, Kyle Lohse, Doug Mientkiewicz, David Ortiz, A.J. Pierzynski

2000s:
Michael Cuddyer, Matt Garza, Francisco Liriano, Joe Mauer, Justin Morneau, Pat Neshek, Wilson Ramos, Denard Span

2010s:
Byron Buxton, David Dahl, Brian Dozier, Ben Revere, Miguel Sano, Trevor Story

too far past that are all sorts of state/legislative buildings.

If you really want to spend more time in central Connecticut, though, you're better off getting back in your car. West Hartford, for example, is a couple of miles down I-84 and has a clean and lively downtown neighborhood.

NYSEG STADIUM

HOME OF THE
Binghamton Rumble Ponies

LOCATION:	Binghamton, NY
TIME FROM:	
SYRACUSE, NY:	1 hour, 15 minutes
ALBANY, NY:	2 hours, 15 minutes
READING, PA:	2 hours, 30 minutes
NEW YORK, NY:	3 hours
PHILADELPHIA, PA:	3 hours
SPRINGFIELD, MA:	3 hours, 15 minutes
OPENED:	1992
CAPACITY:	6,012
TENANTS:	Binghamton Rumble Ponies, Double-A Eastern League (1992–present)
PAST TENANTS:	None
DISTANCE FROM HOME PLATE:	330 feet to left field, 400 to center, 330 to right
RADIO:	1290 AM (Binghamton)

The Triplets' Legacy

Like so many other old northeastern cities, Binghamton dabbled in professional baseball throughout the twentieth century (and even earlier), well before the New York Mets moved the Williamsport (Pennsylvania) Bills to Binghamton for the 1992 season. The Binghamton Triplets—named after the Triple Cities of Binghamton, Johnson City, and Endicott—played in nearby Johnson City from 1922 to 1968, mostly as a Yankees affiliate. Among the noteworthy Triplet alums are none other than Whitey Ford, Thurman Munson, Joe Pipitone, Tony La Russa, and Cito Gaston.

When the Triplets disbanded, however, the old Johnson Field was torn down to make way for a state highway. When the then-Binghamton Mets were born, so was Binghamton Municipal Stadium. It went up in just nine months, forcing the team to postpone only three games at the start of the 1992 season. The park turned into NYSEG Stadium when the New York State Electric and Gas Company bought the naming rights in 2001.

Success came quickly for the B-Mets, now called the Rumble Ponies, both on the field and at the turnstile. For the former, they won the Eastern League championship in that inaugural season, 1992, led by EL Pitcher of the Year Bobby J. Jones, who went on to enjoy a decade-long major leaguer career, mostly with the Mets. For attendance, the B-Mets drew 279,000 in their first year. The good news was that they set a single-season attendance record for any Binghamton baseball franchise. The bad news is that it is still a single-season record for any Binghamton

Past Greats

Here's a partial look at some note-worthy big leaguers who made stops in Binghamton before their major league successes.

1990s:

Edgardo Alfonzo, Jason Isringhausen, John Gibbons (manager), Bobby Jones

2000s:

Jason Bay, Heath Bell, Ike Davis, Lucas Duda, Carlos Gomez, Scott Kazmir, Daniel Murphy, Jon Niese, Angel Pagan, Jose Reyes, Ruben Tejada, David Wright

2010s:

Michael Conforto, Travis d'Arnaud, Jacob deGrom, Jeurys Familia, Wilmer Flores, Matt Harvey, Juan Lagares, Steven Matz, Noah Syndergaard, Zack Wheeler

baseball franchise. Attendance has lagged in recent years as NYSEG has fallen behind its minor league cohorts, but more on that later.

The B-Mets have won the Eastern League twice more: In 1994, a team for which future Met All-Star Edgardo "Fonzie" Alfonzo starred, and in 2014, spurred in part by the late-season and championship-series dominance of left-handed starter Steven Matz.

NYSEG Stadium has also been host of a Double-A All-Star Game (1994) and the site of two B-Mets no-hitters, authored by Joe Crawford (May 5, 1996; seven innings) and Bob Keppel (August 2, 2003).

Bigger and Better Things

Once the beneficiary of the Industrial Revolution, a major production center for shoes and cigars, Binghamton itself isn't what it used to be. Its population peaked around 85,000 in the mid-1950s but was down to about 53,000 when the B-Mets came into existence and is currently down to about 46,000. The city is best known now for Binghamton University, part of the State University of New York (SUNY) system, and a couple of minor league sports franchises, the Rumble Ponies and Binghamton Senators of the American Hockey League.

The neighborhood surrounding NYSEG Stadium isn't great, but is said to be trend-ing upward due in large part to the growth of SUNY Binghamton and the significant student population that comes with it. Parts of downtown Binghamton have already been spruced up, and there are some spots (Little Venice, an Italian joint over on Chenango Street) worth visiting near the stadium.

NYSEG Stadium, a quarter-century old, is ripe for upgrades. As B-Mets general manager Jim Weed conservatively put it, "It is what it is." It's not in bad shape, per se, but lacks some of the bells and whistles of the newer parks, especially those in the Eastern League. A new owner, John Hughes, has spoken about—and indeed begun following through on—improving NYSEG Stadium, so look out for that in the coming years. New in 2017 was a picnic party deck down the right-field line, a third-base terrace for smaller groups, and upgraded stadium lighting—part of a $2.5 million renovation package, with most of that money coming from the state.

Plenty of on-site parking is available for a couple of dollars, which is great. The main seating bowl is similar to many other Double-A parks, split into two levels: box-seat sections closer to the field and reserved grandstand sections above those. They are split by a walkway. Down the right-field line are tables (reservable for small groups, usually birthdays) from which you can nearly touch the field. Down the left-field line is a picnic-buffet area that can accommodate up to 600 people.

The Binghamton franchise, which underwent a rebrand and is known as the "Rumble Ponies" as of November 2016, has designs on bigger and better expansions. There are severe limitations, however, in trying to expand in any particular direction due to the train yard be-

Meet the Mets

For most of this decade, Binghamton has also been a training ground for some of the best New York Mets players to come through the system in recent memory—from its wildly talented rotation (Matt Harvey, Jacob deGrom, Noah Syndergaard) to position players of note (Michael Conforto, Travis d'Arnaud, Juan Lagares). In all, nineteen members of the 2015 National League champion Mets played in Binghamton. The prospecting industry in baseball is impossible to predict, but based on the Mets' general emphasis on player development, it's a safe bet that future stars will continue to grace NYSEG Stadium.

Ballpark Eats

NYSEG Stadium upped its concessions game big time heading into 2016. You can get all of your standard baseball game fare and then some (pulled pork/brisket sandwiches, souped-up nachos, various sausages, and Philly steak items), but the real prize at NYSEG and in Binghamton generally is the *spiedie*. The spiedie is cubed chicken or pork (or lamb) marinated and served on a sandwich roll. If you visit the Southern Tier—the part of New York that runs along the Pennsylvania border—and don't try the spiedie, don't tell any native Binghamtonians. They will look down on you.

You can pick up a spiedie or two at the stadium at Hickory's BBQ stand, located down the first-base line, or the Flash Point Grille, located behind first and third base. Outside the stadium, visit Lupo's S&S Char Pit, a brick-and-mortar restaurant on West State Street in Binghamton, for your spiedie fix.

yond the outfield and streets on other sides of the building. For now, there is no outfield seating and no wraparound concourse, meaning no view of the game while you wait in line for food.

The club has already started to make good on its promise of rejuvenation in terms of the on-field product, installing new grass and outfield walls prior to the 2016 season. There are also plans for new bullpens and batting cages.

The promotional schedule has also benefited from the infusion of energy that has come with new ownership. On the 2016 edition was

a Bark in the Park Night (dogs welcomed, and encouraged) and appearances from the XPogo Stunt Team (pogo-stick experts doing heart attack-inducing tricks), the Zooperstars (inflatable animal costumes that are can't-look-away awkward/funny), and Mr. & Mrs. Met, the parent team's mascots.

Yankee Invasion

A curious—and potentially fun—dynamic at Binghamton games isn't necessarily an obvious one: Despite being a Mets farm team, and despite the Mets' recent success, most of the fans at NYSEG Stadium and in the area generally root for the New York Yankees.

This stems from several factors. First, as mentioned earlier, the Binghamton Triplets (1922–1968) were a Yankees affiliate for most of their existence, and as part of that partnership the parent team played an exhibition game in the Southern Tier every spring, rolling up with all-time greats like Lou Gehrig and Joe DiMaggio. That led to a significant degree of Yankees fandom, which has been passed down through generations. "A lot of people were brought up that way and carried that tradition," says Weed.

Combine that Yankees breeding ground with the fact that the Mets didn't exist until 1962 and were oftentimes unsuccessful in the ensuing half-century. It's been hard for the Amazin's to carve themselves a niche in Broome County, even while having their Double-A team in the city—in part because of the Yankees' considerable success (five World Series titles) in that time.

The bottom line here: You're watching future Mets at NYSEG Stadium, sure, but don't be afraid to wear your Yankees paraphernalia.

Welcomed Stability

Jim Weed heard the whispers. A Binghamton Mets employee since the mid-1990s, and the general manager since 2010, Weed knew all about rumors that the city's professional baseball team would soon leave, rumors that were regular and pervasive, rumors that undermined his ability to do his job. The city was uneasy, wary of supporting a team—a business—that it wasn't sure would exist in a year's time.

Then, with a few straightforward words said with genuine sentiment, a businessman from Georgia lifted that burden, dispelled the rumors, and evaporated the concern and hesitancy. John Hughes bought the Binghamton Mets and, in guaranteeing the club would remain in the Southern Tier, turned into its savoir.

"The B-Mets are here to stay," Hughes, a defense contractor with New York family ties, said at his introductory press conference in December 2015. "Not only for today and not only for the 2016 season, but we're here for the future. There is a long-term commitment in place."

News of that stability spread quickly, and soon Weed heard whispers of a different sort. More happy chatter than whispers, really, townspeople excited and relieved that the team was here to stay. The start of a new era, Weed and others hope, for professional baseball in Binghamton. "I think people took a deep breath," Weed said. "'Okay, good, we're not losing our team." Everywhere Weed went, fans diehard and casual were pumped. "They said, 'Hey, we're so happy the team is staying. We're glad someone stepped up.'" Weed's reaction? "Well, now you have to come to a game."

Challenge seemingly accepted. As a case study, look at the Thursday and Friday heading into Memorial Day weekend 2016, when the B-Mets had their first back-to-back sellouts since 1995. That's in direct contrast to the season prior when, fresh off a championship season in 2014, Weed & Co. expected a bit of an attendance boost. Not so. A couple of days before the season began, there were reports that owners were looking to sell. Attendance had already bottomed out in 2014, when the B-Mets averaged 2,544 fans per game—less than two-thirds of what the team averaged in 1992, its first season.

Now, the trajectory should be upward. The front office knows it'll be a slow climb, that nothing is more valuable than time when it comes to rebuilding trust within the community. It'll take time, too, for Hughes and the club to implement all the changes they would like to, from between-inning entertainment to game-day giveaways to revamping certain sections of NYSEG Stadium.

Stud Muffins?

The most significant of those changes was a complete rebrand. The Binghamton Mets ceased to exist under that nickname once the Name the Team contest finished in the fall of 2016. The finalists? Bullheads, Gobblers, Rocking Horses, Rumble Ponies, Stud Muffins, and Timber Jockeys. The names, which generated nationwide publicity for the team, are goofy and cartoonish, not intimidating or cool. And that's what the B-Mets wanted. The new name, Rumble Ponies, is a nod to the area's rich carousel history.

Weed remembers when other minor league teams that rebranded said, "Trust us, when you roll these names out, people are going to be ornery, they're not going to like it."

"Because it's a shock," Weed explains. "They expect basic sports nicknames, and you're giving them off-the-wall craziness."

In the end, Binghamton hopes, it'll result in more of a hometown identity for the franchise. The "Mets" nickname worked when the team had to establish some legitimacy early in its existence in 1992, but an entire generation has grown up in Broome County since then. It's gotten stale. And these days, more and more farm teams are moving away from sharing the parent team's name. Binghamton is merely jumping on the bandwagon.

"It's been a fun process all around," Weed said. "Some people hate it, but when you explain it to them they start to buy in. "My key thing is I tell them, keep an open mind. Let's keep an open mind and think outside the box and move forward and have fun."

Moving forward and having fun—baseball in general and minor league baseball especially is supposed to be fun, after all—are exactly what Hughes and the new regime want.

How Affiliation Works: An Explainer

People who work in minor league baseball, as they are happy to tell you, can't control two things: the weather and the rosters.

Minor league teams sign a player development contract (PDC) with major league teams in an agreement to become affiliated. This means the parent club will handle the baseball side of the operation (providing the players and coaches), and it's up to the minor league teams to handle the business side (promotions, concessions, in-game non-baseball entertainment).

PDCs usually last from two to four years, but it's common for the parties to re-up before they run out. When a major league team needs a player to replace one who got hurt or cut, they usually call one up from an affiliate.

Every franchise has a farm system—a Triple-A team, a Double-A team, etc.—in which each member is signed to a PDC. Some major league clubs, like the Boston Red Sox and Philadelphia Phillies, try to keep their minor league affiliates geographically close.

Boston has Triple-A Pawtucket an hour south and Double-A Portland two hours north, plus short-season A Lowell even closer. Four of the Phillies' five top farm teams are within a three-hour drive of Philly.

ARM & HAMMER PARK

HOME OF THE
Trenton Thunder

LOCATION: Trenton, NJ

TIME FROM:

PHILADELPHIA, PA: 45 minutes

NEW YORK, NY: 1 hour, 15 minutes

BALTIMORE, MD: 2 hours, 15 minutes

HARTFORD, CT: 3 hours

ALBANY, NY: 3 hours, 15 minutes

OPENED: 1994

CAPACITY: 6,150

TENANT: Trenton Thunder (1994–present)

DISTANCE FROM HOME PLATE: 330 feet to left and right fields, 407 to center

RADIO: 91.3 FM (Trenton)

Rivals Agree

Here's a trivia question for you: What do former Red Sox prospects Nomar Garciaparra, Kevin Youkilis, and Trot Nixon have in common with homegrown Yankees Robinson Cano, Dellin Betances, and Phil Hughes? They all played Double-A baseball in Trenton for the Thunder.

Arm & Hammer Park—originally Mercer County Waterfront Park—represents a fun footnote to the famed Red Sox–Yankees rivalry.

Seeing Stars

Rehab assignments, in which major leaguers get some practice reps with a minor league team as they work their way back from injury, are a familiar occurrence in Trenton, where the Yankees' superstars of superstars briefly suit up for the Thunder. See if you notice a theme in the franchise's top seven attendance marks.

July 3, 2011: 9,212
(Derek Jeter rehab)

May 23, 2007: 9,134
(Roger Clemens rehab)

July 2, 2011: 9,002
(Derek Jeter rehab)

May 10, 2003: 8,729
(Derek Jeter rehab)

May 27, 1998: 8,602
(exhibition vs. Red Sox)

May 9, 2003: 8,461
(Derek Jeter rehab)

May 7, 2003: 8,380
(Derek Jeter rehab)

Trenton was a Boston affiliate from 1995 until 2002, but has partnered with New York since 2003 (when Portland became the Red Sox's Double-A team, a switch that made geographical sense for all parties).

The franchise that is now the Thunder split time between Glens Falls, New York, and London, Ontario, for more than a decade before moving to New Jersey in 1994. The then-new Thunder maintained their affiliation with the Detroit Tigers for one more year before linking up with Boston.

Those past relationships make for a unique blend when it comes to putting the team's history on display at Arm & Hammer Park in the form of photos and occasional bobbleheads. Still a Yankees farm team, the Thunder retired the numbers worn by Garciaparra (Number 5) and David Eckstein (Number 2), former All-Stars who rose through the minor league ranks as Red Sox. Tony Clark, a then-Tigers prospect who was a member of the 1994 Thunder, also had his Number 33 retired by Trenton.

When it comes to on-field team success, the Yankees' Thunder have bragging rights over the Red Sox era, with six division titles to three and three Eastern League championships to zero.

Feel Safe

Trenton, the capital of New Jersey, doesn't have a reputation of being a great place to, you know, hang around and spend a day. Consider Arm & Hammer Park a worthwhile exemption to any sort of why-bother-with-that-city rule or preconception you might have. The stadium is nestled between a highway (Route 29) and a

river (the Delaware), so it's easy in and out if you don't want to loiter.

The immediate neighborhood, too, isn't too shabby. Municipal buildings neighbor Arm & Hammer. The Sun National Bank Center—home through the years to various hockey, lacrosse, and arena football teams, as well as host to concerts and other events—is a five-minute drive away.

As for Arm & Hammer Park itself, maintenance is regular, but it shows its age—specifically, its mid-1990s birth—with a lack of outfield seating. That doesn't interfere, however, with the main seating bowl, which has two levels split by a walkway. Down the left-field line, the Thunder have two picnic areas for groups of twenty or more. They hold a combined 300 people. In the same spot down the right-field line is the kids' zone, highlighted by a popular gigantic version of Connect 4.

At the center of the second-tier suite level is the Yankee Club and Conference Center, a group area that holds up to a hundred people and is the size of three to four luxury suites. The Thunder rent it out on non-game days for company meetings and other get-togethers.

Parking is plentiful. There are four private lots next to the stadium that hold 1,500-plus cars. During fireworks nights—twenty-plus home games per year, usually—the Thunder lose some of those spots, but there is an auxiliary lot a mile down the road. On occasions when that is needed, the Thunder run shuttles to and from.

Trenton's geography makes for quite the blend of major league fans. You get your

Yankees and Mets folks from New York/northern Jersey, but Philadelphia—and thus Phillies fans—is even closer than the Big Apple. Baltimore isn't too far, either. At Arm & Hammer Park, though, they can unite around the Thunder just fine.

Family Business

The Trenton Thunder's occasional national—and even international—publicity has nothing to do with the ballplayers or games and everything to do with a family of adorable golden retrievers who have served as the team's Bat

Ballpark Eats

Trenton, like nearby Lakewood, makes a big deal out of the pork roll—a pork-based processed meat that is pretty much ham—a popular choice in the Philadelphia/New Jersey area. Among the specialty items, pork-centric or otherwise, you'll find at Arm & Hammer are the Swine Sandwich (pork roll, bacon bits, pulled pork), one of a half-dozen pork roll foods; crab fries from Chickie's and Pete's, a Philly-based sports bar; Portobello mushroom, among the healthy options you'll find on the third-base side of the concourse; and local beers from Killarney's On the Delaware, a ballpark version of the bar in Hamilton, New Jersey. If you're looking outside the park, check out Rho Restaurant, a part-dance club and part-pub-style eatery next to Arm & Hammer along the Delaware River.

Dogs since 2002. Here are those words again, in case they didn't click the first time: a family of adorable golden retrievers who have served as the team's Bat Dogs since 2002.

The patriarch of the bat-fetching canines was Chase, who debuted in 2002. He quickly became a fan favorite, running onto the field to retrieve bats after Thunder players' plate appearances the first two innings of every home game. Time took its toll, though, as it does to us all, and the Thunder held a retirement ceremony for Chase in July 2013. The graying and tired golden received one last ovation from the loud Trenton crowd and succumbed to cancer days later.

The Thunder began to wean Chase off Bat Dog duties in 2010, when his son, "Home Run" Derby, got in on the action. He continues to live up to his dad's legacy, bringing umpires water mid-game and generally loving life as probably the most popular living being at Arm & Hammer.

Or, rather, maybe Chase is tied for first in that popularity ranking. Derby's son—Chase's grandson—is Rookie, who was born in late 2013 and joined the family business in 2015. He got his name after a name-the-dog contest on the team's website. Rookie debuted on opening day 2015 and, well, let's just say sometimes rookies aren't quite ready for The Show. Rookie sprinted past home plate and the bat, tripped, and ran around the infield (and then outfield) for a little while before his trainer reeled him back in. All in a day's work.

ESPN's newsmagazine show, *E:60*, featured the Thunder's Bat Dogs in a 2015 story. It's worth checking out, but full disclosure: It's awfully sad. Get the tissues ready.

Other non-baseball attractions at Arm & Hammer include your usual minor league promotions (including bobbleheads of former players, some of them recent former players) and between-inning entertainment (video-board

Past Greats

Here's a partial look at some noteworthy big leaguers who played in Trenton on their way to The Show.

1990s:

Tony Clark, David Eckstein, Adam Everett, Nomar Garciaparra, Shea Hillenbrand, Lou Merloni, Trot Nixon, Carl Pavano, Jeff Suppan

2000s:

Melky Cabrera, Robinson Cano, Francisco Cervelli, Joba Chamberlain, Tyler Clippard, Jorge De La Rosa, Justin Duchscherer, Brett Gardner, Phil Hughes, Austin Jackson, Mark Melancon, Dioner Navarro, David Robertson, Freddy Sanchez, Chien-Ming Wang, Kevin Youkilis

2010s:

Dellin Betances, Austin Judge, Ivan Nova, Gary Sanchez, Adam Warren

Game with a View

The right-field wall is short and has limited ads, in part to offer fans a better view of the Delaware River and, beyond that, Pennsylvania. The water is a popular—and reachable—target for left-handed power hitters. Switch-hitting Tony Clark, the player most of note on the inaugural 1994 Trenton Thunder team affiliated with the Detroit Tigers, was the first batter to hit a ball into the river.

games, dizzy-bat race, mascot race). The Thunder's mascot Boomer, a big blue Thunderbird, almost always loses the mascot race (except on his birthday).

The Thunder in recent years have also created a new tradition: the World Famous Case's Pork Roll Eating Championship, a full-fledged Major League Eating competition hosted at Arm & Hammer in September. Joey "Jaws" Chestnut won both editions through 2016, downing a record forty-three pork roll sandwiches in ten minutes.

FIRSTENERGY STADIUM

HOME OF THE
Reading Fightin Phils

LOCATION: Reading, PA

TIME FROM:

PHILADELPHIA, PA: 1 hour, 15 minutes

HARRISBURG, PA: 1 hour, 15 minutes

TRENTON, NJ: 1 hour, 30 minutes

BALTIMORE, MD: 2 hours

NEW YORK, NY: 2 hours, 15 minutes

PITTSBURGH, PA: 4 hours

OPENED: 1951

CAPACITY: 9,000

TENANTS: Reading Fightin Phils, Double-A Eastern League (1967–present)

PAST TENANTS: Reading Indians, Double-A Eastern League (1952–61; 1965)

Reading Red Sox, Double-A Eastern League (1963–64)

DISTANCE FROM HOME PLATE: 330 feet to left field, 400 to center, 330 to right

RADIO: 1240 AM and 98.5 FM (Reading)

Fabulous 50

The history of FirstEnergy Stadium and those who have played there is as important to the club as anything, and it's easy to see why. Originally Reading Municipal Memorial Stadium, the park was built after World War II in honor of veterans. It is said to be one of the last public projects built under the New Deal. In 2016, the Reading Fightin Phils celebrated their fiftieth

season affiliated with the Philadelphia Phillies. That simple passage of time is irreplaceable when it comes to building a relationship within the community. You can't fake that sort of history.

"There's depth to it," said general manager Scott Hunsicker. "You need someone to build a nice stadium in 1950. You need a franchise to come in 1967. You need a new owner to come in 1987 and invest $20 million. You have to plant the tree."

Added another local and former longtime front-office employee: "All the history that's here, it's a place where grandfathers now came with their grandchildren . . . You don't see that with new stadiums."

The early history of the stadium featured inconsistency. The Reading Indians were the first tenants, and when they bailed after a decade, the Reading Red Sox moved in and lasted two seasons. The Indians came back for one year, then Municipal Memorial Stadium sat empty for a season. The Reading Phillies came to town in 1967, and it's been that way ever since.

After existing as the Reading Phillies for forty-seven years, the club wanted to create its own brand, something that would distinguish it from the Philadelphia Phillies. Reading settled on the "Fightin Phils," sometimes known as simply the "Fightins." The result? Some initial wariness from a fan base resistant to change, followed by a significant spike in merchandise sales and consistently high ticket sales. And, hey, in a few more years, the team can break out the old "R-Phils" stuff and call it retro.

The walls of the main concourse behind home plate serve as a miniature museum documenting all of this history. There are team photos from every season, newspaper clips of opening days, shots of FirstEnergy Stadium then and now, and a list—a very long list—of about 350 former Reading players who reached the major leagues.

Carnival Atmosphere

The Fightins like to think of FirstEnergy Stadium (minus the branded name) as the Wrigley Field or Fenway Park of the minors, that classic American ballpark that is a destination in itself, no matter the quality of team in a given season. History is important to the club, and this park is a big part of that, hence the regular upgrades it has received in the three decades since Craig Stein purchased the team. There are occasional rumors that the Fightins will seek a new stadium elsewhere, but those who spend a lot of time around the team scoff at that idea. Why would they keep putting money into renovations if they wanted to move out?

A revamped main entrance leads right into a plaza/hangout area, complete with concessions, tables, carnival games, mascots, and music. The carnival-like atmosphere is inspired by the Red Sox's Yawkey Way. There is netting

overhead to protect everybody from potential foul balls, and a small stage in one corner is active most days with live music or entertainment. Fightin Phils players have to cross the concourse on the edge of this main pavilion to get from the clubhouse to the field, creating an unusually high degree of access to the players.

As far as seating goes, the options are plenty. You can go to five Fightin Phils games and have five different experiences if you wanted to. The main bowl is the original bowl—the spot from which generations after generations have watched future Hall of Famers take the field. For larger parties, there is the '67 Club picnic area down the third-base line, the deck in left field, the pool pavilion in right, and dugout suites.

The right-field pool is not a misnomer. It is a real, legitimate, heated (86 degrees year-round) pool you can go in. During some early-season (read: cold) games, being in the pool is warmer than being outside the pool. Across the way in left field, a deck area has a bar, group boxes, and a standing-room-only section that is rem-

Cheap Parking

FirstEnergy Stadium is on the outskirts of Reading, not far off the highway and not far from the foot of Mount Penn—a pretty view beyond right field. So while there isn't much to do in the largely industrial neighborhood, the upside is the abundance of cheap or free parking all around.

Ballpark Drinks

The concessions at FirstEnergy Stadium are solid—try the *Churger,* a beautiful chicken patty/cheeseburger hybrid—but the main draw is the significant selection of beer and ciders. Reading is in the heart of craft beer country, and the Fightins tap (get it?) into that.

Yuengling, for example, exploded in popularity several years ago. It's based in nearby Pottsville, and when the Fightins brought it to FirstEnergy, it was a big deal. "It was like the king was in town," said Eric Scarcella, a lifelong Pennslyvanian and the Fightins' PR guru at the time.

Here are three options from which to take your pick of the eighty-seven different beers and ciders at FirstEnergy Stadium: Your Dad's Beer Stand, near the main entrance; Craft Beer Corner, down the third-base line; and Coors Light deck/bar area, in left field.

iniscent of Fenway's Green Monster. The dugout suites are mini-dugouts next to the actual dugouts, spurred into existence by demand for more group seating but a lack of traditional suites. The dugout seating was new in 2016, and sold out almost all year.

Bells and Whistles

FirstEnergy Stadium is the oldest park in the Eastern League, but it has the upkeep to, well, keep up with its younger counterparts. That includes a gigantic—and crystal-clear—video board, new in 2013, in left-center field. And the person or persons who run that video board do brilliant work, from contextually appropriate *Seinfeld* highlights to the popular *Monty Python and the Holy Grail* clip—"Bring out your dead!"—before announcing the visiting team's lineup.

Among the other in-game bells and whistles: Remember Reading Railroad from Monopoly? Blue-collar Reading is known for its railroad industry, of course, and that includes trains running through nearby parking lots during games. In center field, the Fightin Phils have an Exploding Train, which lights up and emits smoke when a Reading runner reaches second or third base, a signal to fans to get loud because the Fightins are trying to make something happen. If and when the runner scores, there are more lights and more smoke, plus fireworks shooting from the smoke stack.

Among the more hilarious—and, to be honest, utterly bizarre—between-innings gimmicks is the Crazy Hot Dog Vendor. Matt Jackson, usually the team's graphics guy, hits pause on those duties during games to run around in a vendor costume while "riding" on a fake ostrich, screaming at the top of his lungs and flinging hot dogs into the stands. It is as ridiculous and fun as it sounds, and the crowd loves it.

A couple of local mainstays worth visiting before or after include Mike's Sandwich Shop on Centre Avenue and Mike's Tavern on Exeter Street. Both are a short walk from the stadium, and they're a block away from each other—but started by different Mikes.

Mornin' Sunshine

Once a year, always on a Monday morning, the Reading Fightin Phils deviate from more than a century of baseball norms with what has become one of the team's most popular traditions: the morning game. Gates open around 7 a.m., the first pitch is thrown at 9:35 a.m., and the game is over oftentimes by noon. It is as unusual a baseball schedule as you will find this side of little league.

The origin story is classic minor league baseball. Every year once the season ends, the Fightin Phils' front office goes on a group retreat to both unwind and look ahead to the next year. Part of that is a half-joking creativity exercise in which staff members write down on separate pieces of paper their best idea and their worst idea, the goal being someone will come up with something the Fightins can work with. That is part of the team's philosophy, which extends from the stadium itself to in-game entertainment to food options: If you're not getting better, you're getting worse.

All of the best and worst ideas are put in one pile and randomly redistributed. Every person has to sell whatever is written down as if it is their own best idea. During the Fall 2001 retreat, one staff member wrote, "Play at 7 a.m. so we can go home early." In trying to sell it, another staff member got pumped: "Let's play at 7 a.m.! In addition to going home early, there are a lot of people able to come at 7 a.m. who couldn't come at other times, like third-shift workers."

Past Greats

Here's a partial look at some noteworthy big leaguers (plus one coach and one executive) who made stops in Reading before their major league successes.

1950s:
Roger Maris

1960s:
Larry Bowa, Rico Petrocelli, Reggie Smith

1970s:
Ruben Amaro, Mike Schmidt

1980s:
Julio Franco, Mike Maddux, Ryne Sandberg

1990s:
Pat Burrell, Mike Lieberthal, Scott Rolen, Jimmy Rollins

2000s:
Michael Bourn, Carlos Carrasco, Cole Hamels, J.A. Happ, Ryan Howard, Carlos Ruiz, Carlos Silva

2010s:
Maikel Franco, Freddy Galvis, Ken Giles, Aaron Nola

That struck Scott Hunsicker, Reading's general manager. Reading, it's worth noting, is an old factory town, more so then than it is now. Hunsicker's father, Tom, worked the third shift his whole life. Scott knew that factory workers, including hundreds of those based out of facilities surrounding FirstEnergy Stadium, treated 7 a.m. as their happy hour. The goofball who

wanted to go home early might actually have been on to something.

Reading played their first morning game the next season. It was a success, but needed tweaking. "The first year we did it, we did it at 9 a.m.," Hunsicker said. "It totally messed up the traffic situation."

The tradition has continued and evolved in the more than a decade since. In 2003, the team moved first pitch to 9:35 a.m. in an effort to avoid the worst of rush-hour traffic. As the city's demographics have shifted—away from factories, mostly—it has become less of an attraction for third-shift workers and more of one for senior citizens who get up early and young kids already out of school for the summer.

In 2016, a whopping 6,305—easily double what could be expected for a Monday afternoon or Monday night game—came to watch a Fightin Phils win. Many of them lined up by 7 a.m. to get that day's giveaway: a bobblehead of Greg Luzinski, a power-hitting perennial All-Star for the Phillies in the late 1970s.

"Definitely early. Different," Reading's first baseman that day, Rhys Hoskins, told reporters afterward with a smile. "But once you get on the field, it's all the same."

In the left-field deck area, a 300-person Kegs and Eggs special sold out. Older fans, in lieu of their mall walk, were allowed to take a "senior stroll" around the warning track. The front office provided players on both teams with breakfast and lunch as a pseudo-apology for messing with their game-day rhythm and routine.

"A little something for the players for the hassle of playing that early," Hunsicker said.

A Cue from Veeck

Years ago, Fightin Phils GM Scott Hunsicker came across a copy of *Veeck—As In Wreck*, the 1962 autobiography of famed baseball promoter and showman Bill Veeck. Veeck is known for gimmicks like Disco Demolition Night at the old Comiskey Park in Chicago or sending 3-foot-7 Eddie Gaedel (jersey number: 1/8) to the plate for a lone at-bat. Veeck also birthed the idea of an early first pitch for a Rosie the Riveter game during World War II.

When he was speaking at a factory during a graveyard shift, a couple of workers complained to him that it was impossible for them to get to any games. So Veeck fixed it with a 9 a.m. first pitch. "All women wearing their welding caps or riveting masks were admitted free," Veeck wrote. "The ushers, in nightgowns and nightcaps, served breakfast: cereal and doughnuts with milk or coffee."

A half-century later, those words brought a smile to Hunsicker's face.

"I was like, 'Wow, we did something Veeck did!'" Hunsicker said. "That's how you know you're doing something right."

The Minor Leagues:
Affiliated Vs. Independent

A common point of confusion when it comes to understanding the world of professional baseball is the difference between affiliated and independent minor league teams.

Affiliated teams—those included in this book—operate under the umbrella of Minor League Baseball, in conjunction with the major league team with which it has a player development contract.

An indy team is, well, independent, operating outside of all that. The Atlantic League and Can-Am League are the two most noteworthy indy leagues in the northeast.

Players with affiliated teams are technically under contract with major league clubs and can thus be promoted to the bigs. Players with indy teams cannot be called up to the majors—unless a team signs them, which does happen rarely (here's to you, Daniel Nava).

The bottom line: If you want to see prospects—the most likely future major leaguers—watch affiliated teams.

That's the point Kevin Kulp, president of the Double-A Harrisburg Senators, tries to hammer home in the team's marketing. Harrisburg has two independent clubs with which to compete, the Lancaster Barnstormers and York Revolution. Both are within forty-five minutes of the Senators.

The Senators, Barnstormers, and Revolution all offer a similar overall product: family-friendly fun and baseball at reasonable prices. But only the Senators can say Stephen Strasburg and Bryce Harper played for them on their way to stardom with the Washington Nationals.

"When you have that level of a prospect that you can hype, it differentiates what is unique about our level of baseball vs. the independent baseball," Kulp said. "Not that they're not doing the same things we're doing—affordable family entertainment—but just that our guys are in a system, and you're looking at future big leaguers."

FNB FIELD

HOME OF THE
Harrisburg Senators

LOCATION: Harrisburg, PA

TIME FROM:

READING, PA: 1 hour, 15 minutes

BALTIMORE, MD: 1 hour, 30 minutes

PHILADELPHIA, PA: 2 hours

WASHINGTON, DC: 2 hours

NEW YORK, NY: 3 hours

PITTSBURGH, PA: 3 hours

OPENED: 1987

CAPACITY: 6,187

TENANTS: Harrisburg Senators, Double-A Eastern League (1987–present)

Harrisburg City Islanders, United Soccer League (2016–present)

PAST TENANTS: None

DISTANCE FROM HOME PLATE: 325 feet to left field, 400 to center, 325 to right

RADIO: 1460 AM (Harrisburg)

Quick Success

The team that became the Senators bounced around small New England towns—Pittsfield and Holyoke, Massachusetts, plus Nashua, New Hampshire—in the 1970s and '80s before making a mid-'80s move to Harrisburg, attracted in part by the promise of a new ballpark. They settled on the Senators nickname in honor of former professional baseball teams in Harrisburg, which themselves drew on Harrisburg's status as the Pennsylvania state capital. Those clubs existed in various capacities and played in various leagues from the late nineteenth through the mid-twentieth centuries.

Once the Senators in their current form moved into a brand-new then-Riverside Stadium in 1987, success was considerable and quick. Harrisburg won the Eastern League in 1987 as a Pittsburgh Pirates affiliate, then dominated in

Home Away from Home

Here's a bit of FNB Field trivia about what didn't happen there: In 2006, during the Senators' twentieth season, they played a pair of home games away from home. Storms flooded the stadium and the neighborhood—and other parts of the city and state—rendering the field unplayable for a couple of days. The Senators and Bowie Baysox played a doubleheader in Bowie, Maryland, about two hours south of Harrisburg. The teams donated half of the proceeds from the games to Red Cross Harrisburg.

the 1990s as a Montreal Expos farm team. They took the title in 1993 and later for four consecutive years, from 1996 to 1999, a highly unusual feat in a game with lots of year-to-year player turnover. The Senators were the Yankees of Double-A baseball, if you will.

River City

FNB Field is tucked away on City Island off the Harrisburg mainland, surrounded by the Susquehanna River—hence the park's original name, Riverside Stadium. The location, between Harrisburg's east and west shores, is convenient accessibility-wise and helps the team avoid a certain stigma. Folks on one side of town don't love going to the other, but City Island is neutral.

The stadium is the crown jewel on the 63-acre City Island, where it's easy to spend most of a day—ballgame or not. With food options, mini-golf, arcade games, batting cages, a walking trail, a beach, the Pride of the Susquehanna riverboat, and a miniature steam train for tours, City Island offers plenty of entertainment options for before or after a game.

During the day, workers from downtown Harrisburg venture across the Walnut Street bridge for a lunchtime walk. Before or after Senators games, fans can venture the opposite way across the bridge to explore the city, including a strip of restaurants on Second Street (two blocks into the mainland) and the Pennsylvania State Capitol complex (a five-minute walk).

As for FNB Field itself, the stadium was built in the mid-1980s, but you'd never know it. Major renovations—about $40 million worth—in 2009 and 2010 modernized the park, and everything except a set of bleachers down the right-field line is new. That includes a high-definition video board in right field, the main seating bowl behind home plate, and the boardwalk-style concourse in the outfield. (More on the boardwalk below.)

The seating bowl, which is mostly covered by a roof, is steeper than similar areas in most stadiums because—being on an island and all—the Senators have to wedge a normal number of seats into a smaller-than-normal plot of land. There wasn't a lot of room to build out, so instead they built up.

Underneath the concourse down the third-base line, there is a kids-centric play area if you raise the white flag on watching the game. As far as group areas go—a specialty for the Senators—there are three options: luxury boxes along the top of the main seating bowl, field-level boxes next to the dugouts, and a large tented area near the right-field corner. The last one is your best bet for large groups. Just on the other side of the foul pole, there is a bar section with a sizable beer selection. Near center, check out Arooga's, part of a regional chain of sports bars with noteworthy wings.

One downside to the older park design: If you want food from the concessions, you have to head down to the concourse, which will rob you of watching the game for however long you're there.

A Bit of the Beach

FNB Field is among the most walkable parks in the region, and one would be wise to wander about over the course of the game to take in as many vantage points as possible. Anywhere in the main seating bowl is an easy choice to start off, but behind/next to either dugout offers a fantastic view and is firmly in line-drive foul-ball territory.

The main in-game draw, though, is probably the outfield boardwalk-style wraparound walkway. The Senators chose that beachy theme for two reasons. First, to avoid floods like the one in 2006. That entire section of building—which includes the front office and ticket window—is up on 12-foot stilts. That way, when it rains, storage areas that can be cleared out are at risk, as opposed to the actual building. Second, the shore, both the Maryland and New Jersey varieties, are popular vacation destinations among greater Harrisburg residents, so the boardwalk serves as the Senators' nod to that.

As for the on-field gameplay itself, you're watching the Double-A Eastern League, so the quality of play should generally be pretty high—and with a regular influx of top prospects. And with the Nationals, whose relationship with

the Senators dates back to the Senators' birth when the Nats were the Expos, there has been a pipeline of young players worth watching over the past decade or so.

Lightning Strikes Twice

In a century and a half of baseball, of the more than 18,000 people who have ever played in the major leagues, none arrived with the same degree of fanfare—and anticipation and attention and excitement and hoopla—as Washington Nationals stars Bryce Harper and Stephen Strasburg.

Harper, the most hyped prospect in the history of the game, and Strasburg, the most hyped pitching prospect, were known names and recognizable faces before they reached The Show, a rarity in a world where most observers don't know the greatness they're seeing until well after it is gone. And in a span of about fourteen months, they both played in Harrisburg.

"Lightning struck twice," said Randy Whitaker, the Senators' general manager.

Strasburg came first. The Nationals made him the number one overall pick in the 2009 MLB draft, a flamethrower out of San Diego State who the club hoped would be an arm they could rebuild the franchise around. Strasburg was advanced enough, even as a new pro, to begin 2010 in Double A—a rare leap.

On April 16, a rainy Friday night after a Thursday home opener the first week of the season, Strasburg was scheduled to take to the FNB Field mound for the first time. Early in the season, with a big prospect debuting, a

Past Greats

Here's a partial look at some noteworthy big leaguers who made stops in Harrisburg before their major league successes.

1990s:

Vladimir Guerrero, Moises Alou, Orlando Cabrera, Cliff Floyd, Matt Stairs, Ugueth Urbina, Jose Vidro

2000s:

Cliff Lee, Ryan Zimmerman, Drew Storen, Jordan Zimmermann

2010s:

Bryce Harper, Stephen Strasburg, Danny Espinosa, Wilson Ramos, Anthony Rendon, Tanner Roark, Trea Turner

recently refurbished ballpark, a crowd of 7,895, "It was a zoo," said one witness. The weather held off, so it was time for the first pitch.

Then the lights went out. But not in any dramatic, time-to-look-at-Strasburg sort of way. It was an actual, unfortunately timed power outage all over the neighborhood.

"The ballpark went dark, and everybody thought, Oh cool, they're going to throw spotlights on him," Whitaker said. "Nope, afraid not. And these lights don't just flip back on like your lights at home. You have to heat them up. So we had to stall to get that done."

Several more minutes of anticipation later, now it was time for the first pitch.

"What I remember most," said Kevin Kulp, the club's president, "is the stillness as he was going into his windup. I don't think the ball ultimately sounded that much different when it went into the catcher's mitt, but the pop—how loud that was, with how still the ballpark was and how quiet it was anticipating that first pitch—was something I'll never forget."

After Strasburg pitched two and one-third innings, the skies opened up. He didn't return after the rain delay, a routine move with a starting pitcher. Most of the fans exited when he did.

Strasburg pitched just twice more at home for Harrisburg, on April 21 and May 2. Those starts came with big crowds, lots of media, and a general sense of excitement that everybody present was seeing something they usually don't. Then he was gone, off to Triple-A Syracuse for a few weeks and the major leagues by June.

The Strasburg Era in Harrisburg, it turned out, was merely a tune-up. The day before Strasburg made his big league debut, the Na-

tionals—again with the number one overall pick—drafted Harper, a seventeen-year-old wunderkind from Las Vegas. This was a kid who, anxious to get going professionally, dropped out of high school to get his GED and enroll at a junior college, which made him eligible for the MLB draft during what would have been his junior year of high school. This was a kid who, at age sixteen, was labeled "The Chosen One" on the cover of Sports Illustrated. Yeah, that kind of hype.

Everything that went into accommodating Strasburg's presence, from ticket sales to extra security to makeshift press conference staging areas, would be needed for Harper's. And that was okay. The Senators had done this before.

"Just off the Strasburg thing, we felt prepared for anything," Kulp said. "And I can't wait, because this is going to be bigger than Strasburg. He's going to play every day."

Harper's first full minor league season, 2011, started in Low-A Hagerstown. Harrisburg was a next step, but no one was sure when he would get there. Then, around 10 a.m. on the Fourth of July, someone from the Nationals called Kulp. Harper was coming. Today.

News spread quickly. In the front office, the phones—all of them—started ringing. People wanted Harper, and they wanted tickets. Kulp called Whitaker, then they called the rest of their employees. With the holiday, everybody was scheduled to come in a little late. Not anymore. At the peak, a dozen and a half members of the front office where answering phones, selling tickets. That still wasn't enough to meet the demand. Official attendance that day: 8,092, edging Strasburg's debut by about 200 bodies.

Mix in the fact that Harper, as an outfielder, would play more or less every day, and his presence generated more excitement than that of Strasburg, who as a starting pitcher stayed on a strict once-every-five-games schedule.

"When the news got out," Whitaker said, "that's when the phone started ringing off the hook."

Added Kulp: "I remember calling everyone on my staff saying, 'Get here as fast as you can.' It turned the Fourth of July into one of those days you'll never forget."

Harper's stay was longer than Strasburg's. He played regularly until mid-August, until an injury robbed him of the end of his regular season. By the next April, a nineteen-year-old Harper joined the Nationals—out west to play the Los Angeles Dodgers—to make his major league debut.

In Harrisburg, he left behind a brief—but memorable—legacy.

"We have lots of great ballplayers who come through here, but you don't know who they are until after they're gone," said Kulp. "Very rarely do you get that guy who's coming through with that level of hype.

"It's never going to happen again. Man, Bryce Harper and Stephen Strasburg came in with such hype. For us to get them in back-to-back years, it was something special."

Ballpark Eats

The FNB Field concessions introduced in 2016 a gigantic, Frankenstein's monster of a sandwich: The R.J. Harrisburger. Named after R.J. Harris, a local radio personality, and the city in which the team resides, the R.J. Harrisburger is an $11 version of a sandwich that concession employees had long concocted for themselves. It's not so much a burger as it is a delicious heart attack in waiting. It includes a half-pound of chopped steak, barbeque pulled pork, pepper Jack cheese, peppers, and onions.

Pro tip: Use a fork.

Minor League Curly Fries

You know that feeling when a curly fry ends up in your batch of French fries, a delicious and welcomed surprise that makes your order a little more worth it? There is a minor league baseball version of that: rehab assignments.

It works like this: When a big leaguer gets hurt and has to sit out for weeks or months or more, he won't return to the majors immediately after receiving a clean bill of health. He has to shake off the rust, work back into game shape. So the parent team will send him on a rehabilitation assignment to a minor league affiliate for a few days. That allows him to take swings and make plays at game speed, but in an environment where wins and losses matter less.

When a major leaguer visits the minors, attention follows. When there is a chance to see an already established star, as opposed to the often-anonymous minor leaguers, fans flock (along with reporters).

Once, in 2011, pitcher Stephen Strasburg and catcher Ivan "Pudge" Rodriguez rehabbed with Harrisburg at the same time. Their presence (plus $2 beer night) made for a much-larger-than-normal crowd of 8,600 at FNB Field. When a visiting Andy Pettitte pitched in Rochester against the Red Wings, it led to the second-largest crowd in the history of Frontier Field, 13,584.

One evening in 2008, news broke that an injured David Ortiz would be playing in Portland in a few days. When employees showed up Sunday morning, they found that their ticket office had had its most successful day ever—on a Saturday night, when no one was there to answer phones.

Pedro Martinez made a stop in Lakewood in 2008 after signing with the Phillies but before returning to The Show. General manager Chris Tafrow, a Yankees fan who never much liked the former Red Sox ace, came away a Pedro fan. "He signed all throughout a rain delay, talked with people, had a good time," Tafrow said. "He really embraced it when he was here."

The wild environment of rehab appearances might be best summarized by a Brooklyn Cyclones executive's take in the summer of 2016. When longtime Met Jose Reyes rejoined the organization and spent a couple of days on Coney Island, it turned a would-be routine week at MCU Park into one that was anything but. "The circus came to town," he said.

PEOPLES NATURAL GAS FIELD

HOME OF THE
Altoona Curve

LOCATION: Altoona, PA

TIME FROM:

STATE COLLEGE, PA:	1 hour
PITTSBURGH, PA:	1 hour, 30 minutes
HARRISBURG, PA:	2 hours
BALTIMORE, MD:	3 hours
PHILADELPHIA, PA:	3 hours, 30 minutes
CLEVELAND, OH:	4 hours
BUFFALO, NY:	4 hours
NEW YORK, NY:	4 hours, 30 minutes

OPENED: 1999

CAPACITY: 7,210

TENANT: Altoona Curve, Double-A Eastern League (1999–present)

DISTANCE FROM HOME PLATE: 325 feet to left and right fields, 405 feet to center

RADIO: 1430 AM (WVAM) in Altoona

Family Business

Bob and Joan Lozinak, Altoona natives who long dreamed of bringing professional baseball to their hometown, first tried to accomplish that goal two decades before the Curve came into existence. In the late 1970s, though, the public support wasn't there, and so they bought a team in Albuquerque, New Mexico, instead.

A generation later, when the town revisited the idea of pro ball as Minor League Baseball was adding teams to account for Major League Baseball's expansion, Bob Lozinak helped lead the charge, eventually securing a Double-A franchise that then worked out an affiliation with the not-too-far-away Pittsburgh Pirates.

The Lozinaks owned the Curve through their first three seasons, but after 2001 sold it to a group of Pittsburgh- and Altoona-area businessmen and athletes, including Pittsburgh Penguins star Mario Lemieux and Pittsburgh Steelers all-pro Jerome Bettis. In December 2008, the Lozinaks and their three sons—Mike, David, and Steve—re-acquired the Curve.

That ownership setup remains, with David Lozinak in particular taking a hands-on role as the chief operating officer, overseeing all day-to-day activity—including, but not limited to, helping out at the concession stands and pulling the tarp before and after rain delays. His brother, Mike, is the club's chief financial officer.

Mother and Father Lozinak very much remain in the picture, too. They forgo use of their owner's suite to sit behind home plate most nights.

Have a Seat

Peoples Natural Gas Field—formerly Blair County Ballpark—is among the fancier parks in the league, despite being in a relatively small market, and features a brick exterior modeled after a railroad roundhouse (in sticking with the train theme).

The seating options are many. The main seating bowl is unusual in that it has an actual upper deck above field-level seats, which gives the place a bit of a major league feel. There are group sections down both lines, with the third-base picnic area serving as the largest option, complete with tents and an exclusive concession stand. The other picnic area is down the right-field line and next to a set of general-admission bleachers and a Kids Fun Zone.

The lone outfield seating is in left, with a large video board and the Lakemont Park property mostly preventing expansion in the other parts of the outfield. The Home Run Junction in left, though, is representative of the team's consistent desire for upkeep. When it debuted last decade, it was among the few sections in

Wild Ride

The ballpark neighbors Lakemont Park, an amusement park with a pair of noteworthy roller coasters. Skyliner is visible from Peoples Natural Gas Field, a can't-miss-it feature beyond the right-field fence. And Leap-The-Dips, built in 1902, is the oldest active wooden roller coaster. Lakemont also has miniature golf, go-karts, paddle boats, and indoor ice skating, so it's easy to spend a whole day at the parks—baseball and amusement.

What's in a Name?

You are forgiven—and not quite wrong—if you assumed the Curve nickname came from the type of pitch. But that's not the main inspiration for the moniker. Altoona is known for its Horseshoe Curve, a nearly 0.5-mile stretch of railroad built in the mid-1800s to help trains navigate the nearby Allegheny Mountains. Rail transport became central to Altoona's identity and economy, and the Curve embrace that theme. Among their mascots? Steamer, a train, and Tenacious, a fierce-looking train engineer. Much of Altoona's pro ball history, which extends back to the late 1800s, follows this theme, including the Rail Kings, an independent team in the 1990s.

all of minor league baseball where fans could sit and catch home runs. (Outfield seating has since become more commonplace.) Beyond the seats is the Hillside Seating—an actual, legitimate hill where fans are free to flock, an especially popular area on busy nights.

No matter where you sit, you can bank on being surrounded by Pirates fans. In addition to the Curve being affiliated with the Pirates, Pittsburgh is also the closest major league city, and central Pennsylvania is thoroughly Pirates country.

The ballpark, close enough to main thoroughfares that you can see it off I-99, is on the outskirts of town, but nothing is farther than a short drive away. The Curve have a parking garage, but when that fills up Lakemont Park has space. It's worth noting that there is

no on-street parking in the mostly residential neighborhood.

If you want to venture into town for something to eat, here's a rule of thumb: If the name of a restaurant is simply someone's name, it's worth a shot. Exhibit A: Tim's American Café, which has big portions at small prices. Also check out Tom and Joe's Diner for breakfast/brunch, and Zach's Sports and Spirits for, well, sports and spirits.

A Word on Attendance

The Curve regularly rank in the middle of the road in the Eastern League for per-game attendance. But when you factor in the town's population—about 45,000 as of 2015, according to the U.S. Census—it's much more impressive. Drawing about 4,800 fans per game in their history, the Curve get about 10 percent of the entire town's population in the ballpark on

Ballpark Eats

The Curve are straightforward when it comes to the concession stands, offering mostly your standard baseball fare and with a couple of less-traditional items (pulled pork nachos, anyone?). The team tends to focus on quality over gimmick. One example: the Curve Burger, a step up from the other burgers offered throughout the ballpark, with high-quality meat and a special bun. It's a premium option, and fans often seek out the Curve Burger specifically when visiting.

any given night. They draw from more than just Altoona, of course, but the population/attendance comparison provides some perspective.

Altoona fans are said to be into the game itself—not always a given at minor league games—so the atmosphere from a pure baseball standpoint is a good one.

Awful Night was Great (and Other Promotions)

The previous ownership group held an annual Awful Night, during which customer service and giveaways and everything except the on-field product (hopefully) was bad. Gimmicks ranged from giving out color photos of the general manager's gallbladder to peanut butter and jelly at the concession stands to displaying the "fail average" (instead of batting average) of hitters.

These days, though, promotions focus on one of two themes: regional ties or Pirates lineage. People from Altoona love being from Altoona, and the same goes for the region generally. In 2015, the Curve hosted A Night in the Neighborhood—specifically, Mr. Rogers' neighborhood. Fred Rogers, the late children's show host, was born in nearby Latrobe, and the team honored him by wearing Mr. Rogers jerseys (think: red sweater, tie). The Curve also had a sweater drive to benefit American Rescue Workers.

The team promotes their alumni, as well as their status as a Pirates farm team, with popular bobbleheads—but always with a twist. Tony Watson's bobblehead, for example, featured him dressed in a trench coat and hat so as to make him look like Mr. Watson, Sherlock Holmes' sidekick. Gregory "El Coffee" Polanco looked like a barista and held coffee. And Starling Marte—whose major league home runs are met with a call of a "Mar-tay par-tay" by Pirates announcer Greg Brown—wore a party hat and held a cake.

The takeaway here: If you want your run-of-the-mill bobbleheads, don't visit Altoona.

Past Greats

Here's a partial look at some noteworthy big leaguers who played in Altoona. The Pirates fan base has a reputation as a hardcore one, and that carries over to Altoona when big-time prospects reach Double A. Over the past half-decade or so, as the Pittsburgh organization has seen an influx of impact homegrown talent, fans have come from far and wide (as far as Pennsylvania goes, anyway) when a much-hyped minor leaguer plays in Altoona.

1990s:
Bronson Arroyo

2000s:
Pedro Alvarez, Jose Bautista, Rajai Davis, Zach Duke, Paul Maholm, Andrew McCutchen, Nate McLouth, Steve Pearce, Ryan Vogelsong, Neil Walker, Tony Watson

2010s:
Gerrit Cole, Tyler Glasnow, Brock Holt, Starling Marte, Jordy Mercer, Gregory Polanco, Jameson Taillon

UPMC PARK

HOME OF THE
Erie SeaWolves

LOCATION: Erie, PA

TIME FROM:

BUFFALO, NY: 1 hour, 30 minutes

CLEVELAND, OH: 1 hour, 45 minutes

PITTSBURGH, PA: 2 hours

AKRON, OH: 2 hours

TORONTO, Canada: 3 hours, 15 minutes

ALTOONA, PA: 3 hours, 30 minutes

DETROIT, MI: 4 hours

OPENED: 1995

CAPACITY: 6,000

TENANT: Erie SeaWolves, Short-Season A New-York Penn League (1995-98) and Double-A Eastern League (1999–present)

DISTANCE FROM HOME PLATE: 316 feet to left field, 400 feet to center, 328 to right

RADIO: 1330 AM (Erie)

Enter "The Uht"

The Erie SeaWolves' path differs from that of most modern minor league teams in that they made a jump up several levels in the late 1990s. Originally brought to town as a member of the short-season New York–Penn League, the Sea-Wolves competed as a Pirates affiliate for four years. After 1998, they became the Double-A Eastern League farm team of the Angels. The strange change means Erie, with 4,200 seats (albeit with a capacity of 6,000), plays in one of the Eastern League's smallest parks.

Do not equate "small" with "bad," though. UPMC Park, renamed after 2016 when the University of Pittsburgh Medical Center bought the naming rights, is a quaint little stadium built into an existing city block just minutes from Lake Erie.

The facility was originally named Jerry Uht Park—or simply "The Uht"—after Jerry Uht, a local businessman who set up an endowment

with the county for small, regular improvements to the park through the years. He also helped bring affiliated minor league ball back to Erie after a one-year absence in 1994. The Erie Sailors, of the NYPL, had existed as an affiliated team from 1932 through 1993, but their owners moved them to suburban New York to become the Hudson Valley Renegades. An independent version of the Sailors played in the Frontier League in 1994. In '95, the SeaWolves were born.

They have played in the years since as part of the farm systems of the Pirates, the Angels and—since 2001—the Tigers, but only yielded so-so on-field results. The SeaWolves have won their division four times, most recently in 2007.

Right-hander Thad Weber tossed on Erie's only Double-A no-hitter on August 22, 2009,

What's in a Name?

You know how parents have a lasting effect on their children? Same thing here. The Pirates were Erie's first parent team, and going on two decades later the SeaWolves maintain elements of the pirate theme. A seawolf is a pirate, the nickname originally borrowed from Pittsburgh's longtime brand. The SeaWolves' mascot, C. Wolf (get it?), is a wolf with an eye patch. Erie sometimes asks its fans, "Arrrr ... you ready for fun?"

throwing just eighty-eight pitches against the Akron Aeros. "I'm not really the kind of guy who sits on the bench by himself," Weber told reporters afterward. "I was up and walking around, trying to talk to everybody, trying to strike up conversations with different guys. But they were just giving me the head nod. I don't think I sat down the last four innings."

Tight Squeeze

One aspect of UPMC Park to note before visiting: It is asymmetrical. Because the park was built into a preexisting city block, it barely fits into the space allotted.

The first-base side abuts 10th Street. There is not enough room for a normal second level, so the grandstands down that line hover over the concourse and the back rows of the field-level seats, resulting in a view that is much closer to the field than a normal upper deck. This raised grandstand was included among the top five in a 2007 ESPN ranking of the best seats in the minors.

Stay Hot

Early-season baseball anywhere in the northeast is potentially awful considering the way spring weather can go. The SeaWolves try to fix this by setting up Heat Zones—large space heaters, essentially—on the concourse down the first-base line, under the raised grandstand seating. This is the only spot in UPMC Park with an open concourse.

Never Forget Your First

The very first game at then-Jerry Uht Park was a memorable one. On June 20, 1995, the Erie SeaWolves beat the Jamestown Jammers on a walk-off home run from right fielder Jose Guillen that is said to have flown over the neighboring hockey arena. The ballpark was jam-packed, too, with 6,300 in attendance that night. Guillen went on to enjoy a fourteen-year major league career with ten teams.

The third-base side has much more space, and thus the grandstands are constructed in a more conventional arrangement.

In that main seating bowl, dugout box seats extend from dugout end to dugout end. Baseline box seats stretch from the dugout ends to the foul poles. All of those sections closest to the field have only six rows, which makes for an intimate experience.

UPMC Park's six suites are situated atop the upper box seats down the third-base line, as opposed to the more traditional spots behind home plate. Picnic areas dominate in the left- and right-field corners. On top of the right-field picnic area are the Bud Light Beer Garden (a bar/hangout area) and Party Deck seats.

There are a mishmash of parking options near The Uht, all of them third-party. The SeaWolves don't own any of it. There are private lots in the neighborhood, a couple of garages, and on-street parking (especially helpful on weeknights when you don't need to feed the meter after a certain hour).

The plus side of having to squeeze a ballpark into downtown is, well, you're downtown. One block west from The Uht is State Street, which has plenty of bars and restaurants. Plymouth Tavern has your typical pub-type food. Cloud 9 Wine Bar is a bit fancier, with a large selection of adult beverages.

Run, Kids, Run!

Getting kids on the field and letting them run around is common in the minor leagues. Getting kids on the field and letting them run around during the game is far less common.

But in breaking with baseball tradition, the SeaWolves created one of their own: the Kids Stampede. In the middle of the sixth inning of every home game, children twelve and younger line up at section 117 (the left-field corner) and sprint across the outfield to section 101 (the right-field corner).

The kids aren't running very far—only a couple of hundred feet—but it can take a couple

of minutes, especially when the SeaWolves get some real tikes out there. The standard break between innings is two minutes and twenty-five seconds, but the SeaWolves applied for (and received) an exemption for this mid-sixth sprint.

There are two other signature Erie promotions worth noting. The first, Buck Night, is an answer to a question many a minor league executive has wrestled with: How do you get fans in the ballpark on Mondays? The answer for the SeaWolves was $1 hot dogs, soda, popcorn, and beer every Monday night game. On warm Buck Nights—far more common in the season's later months—it's normal for 5,000 or so people to pile into The Uht, quite the feat for minor league Mondays.

Howdy, Neighbor

The **Erie Otters** of the Ontario Hockey League play in the Erie Insurance Arena (formerly Tullio Arena), which is not only next to UPMC Park but blatantly visible beyond the left-field fence. In April, when the Otters are competing in their playoffs, hockey season and baseball season overlap, making for quite the busy neighborhood if there are two home games on the same night.

Past Greats

Here's a partial look at some noteworthy big leaguers who played The Uht on their way to the majors.

1990s:
Jose Guillen, Aramis Ramirez, Scot Shields

2000s:
Alex Avila, Curtis Granderson, Omar Infante, Matt Joyce, Jair Jurrjens, John Lackey, Andrew Miller, Fernando Rodney, Bruce Rondon, Cody Ross, Justin Verlander, Joel Zumaya

2010s:
Nick Castellanos, Avisail Garcia, Drew Smyly

A fun dynamic in Erie, as opposed to most other minor league cities in the northeast, is the mixture of major league fans. It is just about as far west as you can go in Pennsylvania, much closer to Cleveland and Detroit than Philadelphia and New York. After the Pirates, the Indians and Tigers are the most popular teams in town.

Ballpark Eats

In addition to your regular options—burgers and tenders, popcorn and cotton candy, beer—the SeaWolves try to work in local specialties and brands. Among your options are pepperoni balls (thinly sliced sausage in deep-fried dough), the Ox Roast Sandwich (roast beef with au jus [think French dip]), and Smith's hot dogs. Smith's, an Erie-based company, is also the "official" hot dog of the NFL's Pittsburgh Steelers and the NHL's Pittsburgh Penguins.

Erie also puts a spin on firework nights, another minors mainstay. Because of the odd dimensions of the ballpark and grounds—again, built to fit into an older neighborhood—the SeaWolves shoot fireworks off from the field, giving fans an unusual perspective on the colored explosives. Fans who buy glow wands and light-up swords on those occasions are allowed to sit in front of the third-base dugout, making the fireworks an even more in-your-face experience.

SINGLE-A
BALLPARKS

FIRSTENERGY PARK

HOME OF THE
Lakewood BlueClaws

LOCATION: Lakewood, NJ

TIME FROM:

TRENTON, NJ: 45 minutes

NEW YORK, NY: 1 hour, 15 minutes

PHILADELPHIA, PA: 1 hour, 15 minutes

BALTIMORE, MD: 2 hours, 45 minutes

HARTFORD, CT: 3 hours

OPENED: 2001

CAPACITY: 6,588

TENANT: Lakewood BlueClaws, Low-A South Atlantic League (2001–present)

PAST TENANTS: None

DISTANCE FROM HOME PLATE: 325 feet to left and right fields, 400 to center

RADIO: 1160 AM (Ocean County) and 1310 AM (Monmouth County)

A Fast Million

First things first: Don't confuse FirstEnergy Park in Lakewood, New Jersey, with FirstEnergy Stadium in Reading, Pennsylvania. (And for that matter, don't confuse either of those with FirstEnergy Stadium in Cleveland, home of the NFL's Browns.)

The BlueClaws moved to Lakewood and FirstEnergy in 2001, after spending about a de-cade and a half in North Carolina under differ-ent names. Since then, they've hosted a South Atlantic League All-Star Game (2002) and won three SAL championships (2006, 2009, 2010) while establishing themselves as one of the best-supported minor league teams in the region and league. They perennially lead the South Atlantic League in attendance, even with their numbers dipping in recent years (down to a still-strong 5,634 fans per game in 2015).

In April 2003, just two-plus years into their Lakewood tenure, the BlueClaws became the quickest SAL club to reach a million fans. A whopping 13,003 of those fans showed up on the same day—August 26, 2002—for . . . no rea-son in particular. It was a nice day out, which helped, and it was the final home game of the season, which is usually a popular choice. Gavin Floyd, then a big-time pitching prospect for the Phillies, was on the mound, and slugger Ryan Howard was in the field. It turned into a perfect storm and an absolute madhouse, a game that lives long in BlueClaw lore.

Aside from that out-of-the-blue huge crowd, the club has taken part in a handful of other curious feats in its relatively brief exis-tence in New Jersey. On July 24, 2002, Floyd threw the team's first nine-inning no-hitter, but lost by a 1-0 final. About a year later, an um-pire ejected groundskeeper Bill Butler from the game, said to be the first time that happened in professional baseball history. In May 2006, Lakewood and Hagerstown played in the lon-gest game in South Atlantic League history, a 22-inning, 8 to 7 BlueClaws win.

Knowing Their Place

What is perhaps the most significant chapter in FirstEnergy Park's histo-ry has nothing to do with baseball. When Superstorm Sandy tore through the area in the fall of 2012, the stadi-um's parking lots turned into a hub for power companies from all over the region who congregated in New Jersey to help. "They built a mini-city like that," said BlueClaws GM Chris Tafrow, snapping his fingers. "It was unbelievable to see."

The ballpark took no abuse, but the BlueClaws knew their place. Peo-ple's lives changed—some of them ruined—over the course of a couple of days. The rebuilding took time, and they wanted to be a part of that. "For us, as a company, we're recreational. When you don't have a house, and I'm calling to see if you want to come to a game, there's a fine line . . . " Ta-frow said, trailing off. Staff members volunteered in neighboring commu-nities, delivering food and gutting houses. "We did what we could do. That year was definitely difficult."

Go Full Circle

What the BlueClaws lack in on-field history—they're only sixteen years old, after all—they make up for with a great facility. FirstEnergy Park is widely considered to be among the best minor league parks in the country, and it leaves little to be desired in terms of game-watching experience.

The neighborhood isn't much. It was woods before the stadium went up, and the neighbors are pretty much just an industrial park. But that's okay, because that means plenty of free parking onsite and nearby, which is needed given how well-attended BlueClaws games typically are.

The ballpark itself feels a lot like the surrounding area: spacious, calm, and still new. The fifteen-section lower seating bowl is the only seating bowl (except for a level of suites), surrounded by a wide and open 360-degree concourse conducive to walking around. Go ahead, do a lap. Rarely in a Single-A stadium will you be afforded that many vantage points.

The outfield offers many of those vantage points. Down the left- and right-field lines are picnic-type areas with tables. In left and right fields—home-run territory—are grassy berms that serve as general-admission sections, allowing the BlueClaws to climb well beyond their 6,588-seat capacity if the need demands it. Next to the berm is an 1,859-square-foot video board, which the team also uses for its Monday Night Movie Series when the BlueClaws are on the road.

The sometimes infamous Jersey Shore is only a ten-minute drive away from FirstEnergy Park—the BlueClaws see an influx from the tourist crowd during the summer months—and the team embraces that beachy atmosphere. The outfield includes a Tiki bar, a couple of lifeguard chairs that fans can climb and sit on, and employees wearing Hawaiian shirts. Riptide, the team's turtle of a mascot, tends to hang out there, too.

League of Their Own

The BlueClaws are different from every other minor league team in the northeast in that they are the only northeastern member of the South Atlantic League. They play clubs as far west as Lexington, Kentucky, and as far south as Charleston, South Carolina, so if your aim is to see as many different franchises or prospects as possible, Lakewood and FirstEnergy Park are your gateway to the 14-team SAL. Take advantage.

The team won recognition in 2015 for their Ball Brawl game, named by Minor League Baseball the best in-game promotion. It's like a capture-the-flag contest, but with the participants running around (and running into each other) in giant bubbles. Hilarity ensues. It was a fan favorite, and by season's end the BlueClaws had other teams calling them to ask how to acquire the inflatable bubbles.

And a quick, lighthearted word on fandom: After about a decade of BlueClaws baseball, a father approached the team's then-general manager. "You did it," he said. The GM wasn't sure what he'd done. The father continued: "You turned my son into a Phillies fan." When the BlueClaws came into existence in 2001, major league allegiance in the area was mostly a Yankees/Mets split (which leaned Yankees). Now, though, the Phillies have wedged their way in there, a generation having grown up watching the likes of Ryan Howard and Cole Hamels play for their hometown team.

Leaving a Legacy

Ask Ryan Howard fourteen years later what he remembers most about playing in Lakewood, and his two answers are nearly immediate.

The first thing Howard says comes to mind is New Jersey's jug handles, the unusual setup on many of the state's roads in lieu of a traditional left-turn lane. Howard, a Missouri boy born and raised, was twenty-two when he ended up in Jersey for his first full professional season. Suffice it to say he did a fair bit of extra driving around before he mastered the jug handles.

"The journey to the ballpark—it was my first time being in New Jersey and driving on the roads. I didn't know about the jug handles to make the left turns," Howard said. "So my first time to the ballpark, I'm following the navigation. I think it was still MapQuest at the time. I'm supposed to make a left here, but there's no left-hand turn. What the hell am I supposed to do?

"So the first couple of times I would go down and try to make a U-turn. Then I learned, okay, the jug handle takes me around."

The second thing Howard remembers has more to do with the atmosphere once he arrived at FirstEnergy Park.

"The biggest thing for me," Howard said, his mouth curling into a smile, "was the crowd."

It would be difficult to forget the people, mostly because there are regularly so many of them. The BlueClaws almost always lead the South Atlantic League in attendance, even if their averages have dipped in recent years (including a per-game average of 5,350 in 2016).

Howard's season in Lakewood—2002—was the BlueClaws' second, and their 6,860 fans per game is the second-best mark in franchise history. That includes the number one all-time single-game gate number of 13,003 in August of that year.

Chris Tafrow, a lifelong New Jerseyan who was then the concessions' manager and has since risen to general manger, remembers that day well. FirstEnergy Park was so busy that when one staffer tried bringing a keg out to an outfield bar area mid-game, he had trouble navigating the packed concourse and dropped the keg on his feet. Tafrow heard the cries for help on his walkie-talkie: "I'm down! I'm down!"

All is well that ends well, though, and that game certainly did. Howard homered, and the BlueClaws won. Gavin Floyd, Howard's fellow 2001 draft pick before they climbed through the minor league ranks together and spent a couple of seasons in Philadelphia as teammates, got the start on the mound for the BlueClaws.

Howard did a whole lot of homering that summer—nineteen dingers in all to go with his eighty-seven runs batted in and twenty doubles (and six triples!). Several years later, the BlueClaws retired his Number 29. Howard and former Philadelphia Phillies ace Cole Hamels (Number 19) are the only BlueClaws to receive that distinction.

Past Greats

Here's a partial look at some noteworthy big leaguers who played in Lakewood on their way to the major leagues.

2000s:

Ryan Howard, Carlos Ruiz, Cole Hamels, Michael Bourn, J.A. Happ, Antonio Bastardo, Carlos Carrasco, Freddy Galvis, Travis d'Arnaud

2010s:

Maikel Franco, Jonathan Villar, Ken Giles

"That's the ultimate honor anywhere," Howard said. "Teams recognizing you enough to say, 'Hey, we feel like you were the best to wear this number, and what you did here was something special.'"

Two years after hanging out in Lakewood, Howard made his major league debut for the Phillies. A year after that, he was the National League Rookie of the Year. Then he won the NL MVP Award in 2005 and helped the team to a World Series title in 2008.

A three-time All-Star in twelve full seasons in Philadelphia, Howard thrice returned to the BlueClaws during major league rehabilitation assignments. He visited in May 2007 with a quad strain, then August 2010 with an ankle sprain. That was when the team retired his jersey number. Howard's most recent trip back to Lakewood came in June 2012 as he worked his way back from offseason Achilles tendon surgery.

Each time, the memories came flooding back, aided by larger-than-normal crowds delighted to see a Phillies superstar and the first BlueClaws alumnus to play in the big leagues (edging Floyd by two days).

"You have a lot of the memories from when you played there originally," Howard said of those rehab games. "It makes you reflect on the road that you've taken to get to the big leagues. Having people appreciate what you did when you were there and what you've done to get up [to the majors] is awesome.

"It's kind of like they grew with you. The cities, all the minor league cities you've played in, the teams I played for, that's a part of me. That's a part of my journey. That helped me grow and become the ballplayer I am."

CENTENNIAL FIELD

HOME OF THE
Vermont Lake Monsters

LOCATION: Burlington, VT

TIME FROM:

MONTREAL, Canada: 1 hour, 45 minutes

MANCHESTER, NH: 2 hours, 30 minutes

ALBANY, NY: 3 hours

BOSTON, MA: 3 hours, 15 minutes

NEW YORK, NY: 5 hours, 30 minutes

OPENED: 1906

CAPACITY: 4,415

TENANT: Vermont Lake Monsters, Short-Season A New York–Penn League (1994–present)

PAST TENANTS: Vermont Mariners, Double-A Eastern League (1988)

Vermont Reds, Double-A Eastern League (1984–87)

Burlington A's, Class C (1955)

University of Vermont Catamounts: (1906–2009, with occasional gaps)

DISTANCE FROM HOME PLATE: 330 feet to left field, 405 to center, 325 to right

RADIO: 960 AM (Burlington)

A Delicate Balance

The most common adjective used to describe Centennial Field? Historic. More than a century old, Centennial was originally constructed as part of the University of Vermont's centennial (get it?) celebration and expansion, which included other sports facilities.

The UVM Catamounts baseball team called Centennial Field home for more than 100 years—with breaks during World War I, World War II, and most of the 1970s—until the school cut the program in 2009. Since then, it's been all Lake Monsters, who have become largely responsible for upkeep.

With that comes a difficult balance: trying to maintain the character and history of the ballpark while keeping up as best as possible with the twenty-first century. In a battle of frills versus charm, the latter usually wins out.

There have been plenty of upgrades this decade, however, at the expense of owner and president Ray Pecor, a Burlington businessman who helped bring the team to town in the early 1990s. Among the first renovations were new home and visiting clubhouses, plus a new infield playing surface—changes that don't mean much to fans, but were important to keeping Centennial workable as a minor league home.

The Lake Monsters followed by making considerable alterations in advance of 2013. They moved the backstop closer to home plate to make way for more seats and made a Family Fun Zone down in the right-field corner. Fixed seats replaced the hard concrete general-admission grandstands. The previously bumpy road leading to the ballpark got repaved. All of those fixes joined the new video board and light towers, themselves only a couple of years old.

Everything's Close

Centennial Field is beautifully low maintenance, a stripped down and less commercialized version of America's pastime. There are ten sections from which to choose. Sections A through D are behind home plate, between the dugouts. Sections 101 through 103 extend from the start of the dugout to about first base, and Sections 301 through 303 do the same on the third-base side. In left field are the video and scoreboard; in right you'll find the away and home bullpens—new features this decade after the most recent renovations.

There are no suites at Centennial Field. The only explicit group area is down the left-field line, a BBQ/picnic section with a serving tent and numerous tables. Across the way along the right-field line the kids' zone neighbors the Vermont Frames Pavilion & Bar, which seems

Buck Well Spent

The Lake Monsters are a relatively small operation, and for a little while this century they battled year-to-year financial/facility uncertainty. The team and the University of Vermont, which still owns the field, helped quell long-term fears when in 2012 they agreed to a twenty-year lease, during which the Lake Monsters will pay UVM $1 per year for use of Centennial Field.

like an awfully convenient setup for parents with children.

The recent renovations took a big bite out of Centennial's foul territory—a change that allows fans to sit closer to the action, even if it isn't to the pitchers' liking. That is true down both foul lines, as well as behind home plate. The Diamond Deck seating area is a 100-person section directly behind the backstop.

Like it is in many decent-sized cities, parking is a bit of an issue at Centennial Field. Lake Monsters General Manger Joe Doud called it the team's number one challenge. There are about

Historical Expo-sition

After the Montreal Expos—formerly Vermont's parent club—moved to Washington, D.C., and became the Nationals for the 2005 season, the then-Vermont Expos in 2005 became the last professional baseball team to play under the Expos nickname. More than a decade later, the team continues to have a fan base that is partly Canadian, despite (or maybe because of) being an hour from the Canadian border.

200 spaces near Centennial, with some close by satellite parking. The big lot—a 5,000-space garage on the heart of UVM's campus—is about a mile away. The Lake Monsters run shuttles to and from so fans don't have to walk.

Past Greats

Here's a partial look at some noteworthy big leaguers who played in Centennial Field. For simplicity's sake, we'll limit this list to affiliated professional baseball, as opposed to players from UVM and other summer collegiate action hosted in Burlington.

1980s:

Ken Griffey Jr., Lenny Harris, Barry Larkin, Lloyd McClendon, Paul O'Neill, Chris Sabo, Omar Vizquel

1990s:

Geoff Blum, Milton Bradley, Orlando Cabrera

2000s:

Jason Bay, Ian Desmond, Marco Estrada, Sandy Leon, Derek Norris, Jordan Zimmermann

2010s:

Addison Russell, Ryon Healy

It's worth noting that the list of noteworthy alumni from the 2010s could and should grow in the coming years. Players in the short-season New York–Penn League are—if they take a traditional route through the minors—five promotions away from reaching the big leagues, so it can easily take a half-decade.

As for Burlington overall, it's definitely a college town—with the University of Vermont and Champlain College right there in town and others not far—but all that means for Lake Monsters season is unusual quiet. The New York–Penn League doesn't start until mid-June, when the college kids are largely gone, and wraps up in early September, around the time they come back.

Burlington, too, is very much typical Vermont—in the best way possible. Farm-to-table is a staple in local eateries, made easier by the significant farmland surrounding the city. The area's microbrewing industry is booming, highlighted by Heady Topper in nearby Waterbury.

If you're looking for dinner somewhere other than the ballpark, try Guild Tavern in South Burlington. If you're looking for breakfast or lunch, hit up Henry's Diner, which is about five minutes from Centennial and even closer to Lake Champlain.

Hot Diggity Dog

If you are going to venture all the way up to this-is-pretty-much-Canada northern Vermont, try to make it during one of the Lake Monsters' 25-cent hot dog nights, easily the team's most successful promotion. The gimmick is pretty self-explanatory: give a quarter, get a hot dog.

The Lake Monsters have quarter hot dog nights about three times a year. During the last of those in 2016, they broke their record by selling 9,400 tubed meats. That's about 39 per minute—one hot dog every second and a half, for four consecutive hours!—and more than two per person for a sold-out crowd.

"We have it down to a science," Doud said.

He's not kidding. In the week leading up to quarter hot dog night, the concessions folks load up on product orders. That's not only hot dogs and buns, but condiments too. The day of, prep work starts around noon for a 7 p.m. game. The crew—bolstered to a larger-than-normal staff—pre-splits about 6,000 buns. That helps them stay on top of the demand once the gates open around 6 p.m.

The Lake Monsters' hot dog provider, the Burlington-based McKenzie Country Classics, brings in a portable extra concession stand strictly for hot dogs. Lake Monsters staffers wander the concourse handing out condiments.

The revenue at night's end is great, sure, but the in-game attendance and atmosphere are also superb.

Other than that—do you need more than twenty-five-cent hot dogs?—the Lake Monsters' promotional schedule is a wee bit different than that of most minor league teams. Bobbleheads, Doud noted, don't really move the needle, so the team moved away from those years ago.

Instead, the Lake Monsters focus on more Vermont-centric giveaways. That could mean anything from free road jerseys (with "Vermont" sprawled across the front instead of "Lake Monsters") to working with Burton, the skiing/snowboarding company headquartered in the city, to give out backpacks.

What's in a Name?

Among the 30,000 entries to a name-the-team contest when Vermont needed to move away from the Expos moniker were Green Mountain Boys, Maplebombers, Foliage, Jee-zum Crows, and Howlin' Howards—the last of those inspired by the former Vermont governor, Howard Dean, and his infamous scream.

The club ultimately went with Lake Monsters, after the Loch Ness Monster-esque—"mythological or possibly real, depending on who you're talking to," as Doud put it—said to live in Lake Champlain. The Lake Monsters' mascot, Champ, also draws its name from the creature.

LELACHEUR PARK

HOME OF THE
Lowell Spinners

LOCATION: Lowell, MA

TIME FROM:

BOSTON, MA:	45 minutes
MANCHESTER, NH:	45 minutes
PORTLAND, ME:	1 hour, 45 minutes
HARTFORD, CT:	1 hour, 45 minutes
ALBANY, NY:	2 hours, 45 minutes
NEW YORK, NY:	4 hours
MONTREAL, Canada:	4 hours, 30 minutes

OPENED: 1998

CAPACITY: 5,030

TENANT: Lowell Spinners, Short-Season A New York–Penn League (1998–present) UMass-Lowell River Hawks, NCAA Division 1 America East Conference (1998–present)

DISTANCE FROM HOME PLATE: 337 feet to left field, 400 to center, 302 to right

RADIO: 980 AM (Lowell)

Tough Ticket

When the Elmira Pioneers bailed on New York's Southern Tier in the mid-1990s in favor of a suburb north of Boston, the newborn Lowell Spinners and the Boston Red Sox made the smart marketing move of partnering up. If there were growing pains, well, they didn't last long.

The Spinners played at Stoklosa Alumni Field for their first two seasons, 1996 and 1997, while the more permanent Edward A. LeLacheur Park was built. The Spinners moved into LeLacheur (La-lash-er) for 1998. In 1999, they began a sellout streak that lasted more than a decade.

Again: a sellout streak that lasted more than a decade.

"We created a monster," said Shawn Smith, the Spinners' president and general manager for most of that run.

On August 3, 1999, the Spinners sold out LeLacheur, then did so repeatedly throughout the month. In 2000, they sold every seat all season, becoming the first team in 120 years of minor league baseball to do so. Then they

did it again in 2001 and 2002 and 2003 . . . and 2004 and 2005 and 2006 and so on, buoyed by a baseball-loving population, a strong promotions game, and a series of exciting Red Sox prospects. It helped that the parent club was also very successful, winning two World Series over the course of the Spinners' streak.

Demand for tickets got to the point where by the time individual games went on sale—after season-ticket holders and large groups got dibs—fans would camp out around the ballpark for ten-plus hours to try to secure seats. That happened in March, when New England is usually still very much enduring winter.

What's in a Name?

Are you mentally prepared for flashbacks to eighth-grade history class? Lowell, with its miles of canals and numerous textile miles, played a key role in the Industrial Revolution. "Spinners" is a reference to the mill workers who turned raw cotton into fabric. The team's logo used to be a spool of thread wrapped around a baseball bat.

The Spinners also set up a promotion where, if you bought a $4 standing-room-only ticket, you could keep your eye on seats unoccupied by the usual season-ticket holder. If it was still empty by the end of the second inning, it was all yours.

The streak ended on August 30, 2010. It lasted 413 games and 4,045 days.

That's when Lowell ran into an issue. For years, Spinners tickets were near-impossible to get, and when the streak ended—when tickets were indeed available—their unattainable reputation remained. People thought they couldn't get into LeLacheur, so many didn't try. Average attendance dipped to 4,600 in 2011, still almost a sellout. But the Spinners didn't pack LeLacheur to a SRO capacity like they did in the halcyon days of yore.

Now the Spinners are working to re-fill LeLacheur like they used to. Attendance in 2016 was 3,782 fans per game.

Little about LeLacheur Park has changed over that time, of course. It's still a clean, quaint stadium on the banks of the Merrimack River—the same river that goes by the New Hampshire Fisher Cats' home—in the heart of the University of Massachusetts campus in the city.

Have a Seat

The Spinners and Red Sox maintain a degree of synergy rare in the minor leagues. It helps, of course, that LeLacheur Park and Fenway Park are only 33 miles apart.

Lowell adopted Boston's color scheme (mostly red and blue). The Spinners placed their large scoreboard—40 feet high at its

YEP? YES

The Spinners earned national headlines in 2006 by helping solve a problem that tormented youth baseball and softball players all over New England: playing for the "Yankees." In local youth leagues, which often borrow major league team names for their own, getting assigned to the Red Sox's hated New York rival was brutal.

The Spinners offered free uniforms, equipment and the chance to play at LeLacheur Park to any league that dumped the Yankees name in favor of the Spinners'. The program was an immediate success and lasted for more than a half-decade.

peak—in left field to give LeLacheur a bit of a Green Monster feel (though Lowell's monster electronic isn't quite as long as Boston's wall). LeLacheur is 302 feet down the right-field line, just like Fenway. And the Spinners, like the Red Sox, display Boston's retired numbers in right field.

When the Red Sox removed the giant Hood milk jug from right field, it ended up in Lowell. Same goes for one of the two Coke bottles that used to sit atop the Green Monster.

It all combines to give LeLacheur Park a distinct Fenway feel.

Incidentally, that extends to the fact that it's hard to get around parts of LeLacheur (and the more than century-old Fenway). You enter at street level, but immediately have to walk up a set of stairs to get to the rest of the stadium.

What's in a Name? (Part II)

The Spinners have thus far avoided the industry norm of selling the naming rights to their ballpark. Instead, LeLacheur Park is named after Edward A. LeLacheur, a longtime state representative who was key in securing the state funding that helped build the stadium. Lowell born and raised, LeLacheur died in August 2010.

Once you reach the concourse level, though, the rest of is easy. The concourse is open and spacious. LeLacheur's main seating bowl is broken up into three price points: premium box seats, box seats, and reserved seats. The last option, benches with backs, is farthest from the action. Wherever you sit, you can see the distinct Aiken Street Bridge beyond right field and the sunset—when the timing and weather is right—beyond left.

LeLacheur Park does not have any outfield seating, but check back on that in the coming years. The Spinners have designs on a right-field party deck.

Lowell is urban, but the amount of parking available is usually plenty, between a couple of lots just east of LeLacheur and a garage to the west. The city overall can get a bit of a bad rap, but LeLacheur's neighborhood at least it isn't deserved. UMass-Lowell, including dorms where Spinners players live in the summer, and luxury condos are in the immediate vicinity.

Lowell is a sneaky-good food town, too. Bani (Dominican) is within walking distance, and Marko's (Greek/Mediterranean) is a short drive. The nearby Owl Diner (breakfast/lunch) is a Lowell staple.

Bobblehead Legacy

More so than with most teams, the Spinners boast a long and creative bobblehead history, typically as giveaways to the first predetermined number of fans to show up to the selected game. Those honored with a large-headed figurine made in their likeness are often—but not always—former Spinners or Red Sox or both.

Here are some of the off-beat bobbleheads, all of which uphold the local theme.

Jack Kerouac: A Lowell native, Kerouac was a football star for Lowell High in the 1930s. The Spinners have honored the leg-

Ballpark Eats

First things first: LeLacheur Park has a full liquor license. That means mixed drinks, not just beer. Food-wise, the Spinners stray a bit from baseball norms by trying to work in healthy options—salads, wraps—in addition to your regular ballpark fare, which includes Sal's pizza, made by hand on-site; cheesesteaks; and fried dough.

Past Greats

Here's a partial look at some noteworthy prospects who played at LeLacheur Park on their way to big league success.

1990s:
Adam Everett

2000s:
Clay Buchholz, Jacoby Ellsbury, Jed Lowrie, Justin Masterson, Brandon Moss, Jonathan Papelbon, Hanley Ramirez, Freddy Sanchez, Christian Vazquez, Kevin Youkilis

2010s:
Andrew Benintendi, Mookie Betts, Jackie Bradley Jr., Jose Iglesias, Travis Shaw

endary writer thrice, including once in his Lowell football jersey.

Paul Revere: The Revolutionary War hero didn't have any direct Lowell ties, but New England never misses a chance to talk about or show off its Colonial history.

Tom Glavine: The Hall of Fame pitcher, who grew up in nearby Billerica, might be the best baseball player from Massachusetts of all time.

Rick and Dick Hoyt: The father and son are Boston-area celebrities. Rick, the dad, pushed Dick, the son who has cerebral palsy, and his wheelchair through thirty-two Boston Marathons.

John Kerry and Scott Brown: The Spinners honored Kerry and Brown, at the time Massachusetts' senators, a week apart in August 2010.

JOSEPH L. BRUNO STADIUM

HOME OF THE
Tri-City ValleyCats

LOCATION:	Troy, NY
TIME FROM:	
HARTFORD, CT:	1 hour, 45 minutes
SYRACUSE, NY:	2 hours, 15 minutes
BOSTON, MA:	2 hours, 45 minutes
NEW YORK, NY:	2 hours, 45 minutes
MANCHESTER, NH:	3 hours, 15 minutes
PHILADELPHIA, PA:	3 hours, 45 minutes
OPENED:	2002
CAPACITY:	4,500
TENANT:	Tri-City ValleyCats, Short-Season A New York–Penn League (2002–present)
DISTANCE FROM HOME PLATE:	325 feet to left and right fields, 400 feet to center
RADIO:	Online

Home Sweet Home

There is no official record for shortest geographical minor league moves, but the Tri-City ValleyCats are probably among the leaders. The old Pittsfield Mets (1989–2000)/Astros (2001) packed up their Western Massachusetts abode and moved less than 40 miles northwest to Troy, New York, in time to play the 2002 season at the brand-new Joseph L. Bruno Stadium—better known as "The Joe."

And that is where the ValleyCats have remained, through seven division titles (2004, 2006, 2010, 2012, 2013, 2014 and 2015), two NYPL championships (2010 and 2013) and more than 2 million fans over fifteen years.

The attendance marks at Bruno Stadium have been something to behold. The ValleyCats broke their own gate record nine years in a row, from 2004 to 2012, and even though attendance has bobbed in recent years—as is often the case when the shine of a new ballpark wears off a bit—Tri-City remains among the NYPL leaders annually. In 2016, that meant an average of 4,281 fans per game—about 95 percent of the stadium's capacity.

One secret to the ValleyCats' success, besides a regular stream of impact players and, in turn, on-field accomplishments, is that any given game at The Joe is different than every other game. Tri-City boasts thirty-eight different themed nights, one for every home game in a season—Irish Night, Military Appreciation Night, Christmas in July, '60s Night, 50-cent Hot Dogs Night, Star Wars Night. There is also "Dark Tuesday: Track Night," when the ValleyCats try to take advantage of Saratoga (Horse) Race Course being closed.

The list of Tri-City's theme nights goes on, of course, and most are designed to get different segments of the community—say, Union, RPI, and Albany Devils fans on Hockey Night—into The Joe.

Have a Seat

Bruno Stadium, built on Hudson Valley Community College's campus, won't overwhelm you with seating options. Fans walk in at street level, which is also concourse level, and the lone tier of the main bowl slopes downward toward the field, which is set into the ground. That—along with the wide, open-air concourse—is indicative of the ballpark's relatively young age.

Ticket prices are based on proximity to home plate. Premium box seats extend from third to first base, and reserved box seats from the shallow outfield to medium-depth outfield. A couple of grandstand sections reach to just about the foul poles. Another twenty-first-

What's in a Name?

Why "Tri-City"? Troy combines with Albany and Schenectady to create New York's "Capital Region." It made more sense from a marketing standpoint to be inclusive of the whole area instead of just Troy, the smallest of those three cities. Albany is a couple of miles from The Joe and about twenty minutes from Schenectady.

And a ValleyCat is a mythical bobcat-type feline that lives in the Hudson Valley. Unlike New Hampshire's Fisher Cats, it is not real.

¡Vamos Gatos!

The ValleyCats' popular rallying cry/slogan, "Vamos Gatos," started a few years ago when former manager Ed Romero heard one of his players say it. He made it a thing, and soon it caught on with fans. Now it's a hashtag and all over t-shirts. The phrase translates from Spanish to "Let's go Cats!" Albany County has a growing Hispanic population, and about one-third of the ValleyCats players every year speak Spanish.

century amenity not to take for granted: the seats are wide, and all have seatbacks.

There are a handful of group sections, besides the ten luxury suites that hang above the concourse. The Top of the Hill Bar & Grill is probably the most popular, offering an elevated view of the field at the actual top of an actual hill. The Picnic Pavilion down the right-field line is another option, and The Porch is a two-tiered wooden deck in the right-field corner. The Porch and The Top of the Hill neighbor grassy berm areas.

The Joe has plenty of parking, in part because it is on a college campus and the ValleyCats play during the summer, when the school is mostly quiet. None of the five main lots are more than a short walk away from the stadium.

Troy as a whole is said to be increasingly nice, with the downtown area in particular getting a lot of hype and drawing comparisons to Brooklyn. The city sits along the Hudson River and is home to Rensselaer Polytechnic Institute.

Hometown History

The Capital Region has a long baseball past, including a major league team, the Troy Trojans, who competed in the National League from 1879 to 1882.

The ValleyCats honor that history with their annual Capital Region Baseball Heritage Night, when they give out bobbleheads of a baseball player with local ties. That includes a bunch of the Double-A Albany-Colonie Yankees (Derek Jeter, Mariano Rivera, Bernie Williams, Andy Pettitte, Jorge Posada), some of the famous former ValleyCats (Dallas Keuchel), and even one early twentieth-century ballplayer, Johnny Evers, of "Tinker to Evers to Chance" fame. Evers was born in Troy and played for the Class B Troy Trojans in 1902.

Local Matters

The ValleyCats put an utterly brilliant, Capital Region–specific spin on the mascot race, a common between-inning gimmick. Like Washington's presidents and Milwaukee's sausages, Tri-City has its mayors, one each from Troy, Albany, and Schenectady. Staffers dressed up in large-headed mascot costumes designed after the real-life mayors of those towns race around the warning track at every home game. Sometimes, when the actual mayor is in attendance, he or she will get involved.

One thing the team didn't consider when it came up with the idea a few years ago: the frequency with which towns get new mayors.

The ValleyCats are up to seven costumes in all, three active and four retired.

"We have a whole closet full of former mayor giant heads," General Manager Matt Callahan said.

That is the sort of thing the ValleyCats do to endear themselves to the community, along with locally based concessions and locally inspired promotions and giveaways.

Tri-City also tends to be involved on the community service front, with one particularly noteworthy tradition: The Community

Past Greats

Here's a partial look at some noteworthy big leaguers who have played at The Joe in its short history. The ValleyCats display photos of every alum who makes it to the majors on their "Joe to The Show" wall.

2000s:

Matt Albers, Jose Altuve, Chris Johnson, Dallas Keuchel, J.D. Martinez, Bud Norris, Hunter Pence, Ben Zobrist

2010s:

George Springer, Vince Velasquez

One other player who isn't significant on his own but could be in the years to come: Daz Cameron, the son of longtime big leaguer Mike Cameron, who played for the ValleyCats in 2016. The Astros picked him in the first round of the 2015 MLB draft.

Also from the famous sons department: One of Roger Clemens' kids, Koby Clemens, played briefly for Tri-City in 2005.

Grounds Crew. For years, the ValleyCats picked one youth baseball field per year and completely re-made it—new infield grass, a rebuilt pitcher's mound, fixed up baselines. At the start of this decade, they decided to up their game with the "4 in 24 Extreme Field Renovation Project," in which they renovated four fields in twenty-four hours.

Ballpark Eats

The ValleyCats run their own concession stands as opposed to outsourcing them to a third party. As a result, they have lots of flexibility. They incorporate a bunch of local places—including Brown's Brewing Company, which has a Troy location—and tend to use the kiosks as specialty stands, each with a certain theme.

Check out Left Field Louie's for wood-fired pizza, made on-site, and pulled pork sandwiches; Tiki Hut for margaritas and beer; Sweet Tooth for ice cream and candy; Helmbold's Corner for hot dogs and sausages; and Vamos Tacos for tacos, burritos, and nachos.

What To Watch For: Prospects

Minor league baseball is a great way to have a relaxed night out or to spend an afternoon with your young children. But if you're a more serious baseball fan—ignoring the mascot races and T-shirt tosses and maybe beating traffic instead of sticking around for fireworks—chances are you want to know which players to make note of.

Fortunately for you, public interest in prospects has boomed in the twenty-first century. And thanks to the internet, plenty of information and scouting reports are available. There are three media outlets that should be your go-tos:

- **BASEBALL AMERICA:** Founded in 1980, BA publishes annually its "Prospect Handbook," complete with top-thirty rankings for every organization and more information than you'll know what to do with. Online, BA does top-ten lists for each farm system and updates its top-100 overall list midseason. BA's in-season minor league and amateur coverage is thorough, too.

- **BASEBALL PROSPECTUS:** Similar to BA, BP's eponymous book includes its top 101 prospects. Its website, much of which is behind a paywall, includes team top-ten lists and midseason updates.

- **MLB.COM:** The official website of Major League Baseball beefed up its prospect coverage a few years ago, and given its thoroughness (very), cost (nothing), and design (user-friendly), it might be the best option of the three. "MLB Pipeline," as it's called, does top-100 overall rankings in addition to top-thirty lists for every team and top-ten lists for every position.

It's also worth looking for team-specific minor league websites. SoxProspects.com, for example, is a must-visit before checking out any Red Sox farm team.

The downside to increased attention on prospects is the increased hype—and, inevitably, failure to live up to the hype. Remember that an overwhelming majority of pro baseball players never make it to the majors, and even the surest of Next Big Things are no sure thing.

LEO PINCKNEY FIELD AT FALCON PARK

HOME OF THE
Auburn Doubledays

LOCATION:	Auburn, NY
TIME FROM:	
SYRACUSE, NY:	45 minutes
ROCHESTER, NY:	1 hour, 15 minutes
ALBANY, NY:	2 hours, 30 minutes
PHILADELPHIA, PA:	4 hours, 15 minutes
HARTFORD, CT:	4 hours, 15 minutes
NEW YORK, NY:	4 hours, 15 minutes
OPENED:	1995
CAPACITY:	2,800
TENANT:	Auburn Doubledays, Short-Season A New York–Penn League (1995–present)
DISTANCE FROM HOME PLATE:	330 feet to left and right fields, 400 to center
RADIO:	98.1 FM and 1590 AM (Auburn)

Demolition Derby

At the end of the 1994 season, with the original Falcon Park as decrepit as ever and about to be replaced by a new stadium with the same name, Auburn town and team officials faced two issues.

The first was the logistical hurdle of building a ballpark on a tight timeline, in a part of the country where winter comes early and stays late. The second was skepticism within the community that Falcon Park I, an unimpressive facility that had nonetheless been a part of Auburn for generations, would really give way to a newer version of itself.

The solution to both problems: Begin demolition of the original Falcon Park immediately after the final out of the final game.

Unattached

For three years, from 1978 through 1980, Auburn played under three team names (Sunsets, Red Stars, Americans) as a co-op team, receiving minor leaguers from a several major league clubs instead of operating under a player-development contract with just one—an unusual setup these days that was more common at the time. Those rosters featured a combined four players who eventually made the majors. Auburn went 83-130.

The Americans folded after 1980, and Auburn endured a one-year hiatus without pro ball. The Auburn Astros were born in 1982 and rebranded as the Doubledays in 1996.

Shawn Smith, a longtime minor league sports executive who at the time served as Auburn's general manager, laughs at the memory more than two decades later. He remembers it going like this: Before the last game, they compromised the integrity of one section of the outfield wall, so as to make it easier to fall down. They also positioned a bulldozer on the other side of the fence for a sneak attack when the time was right. Seconds after a postgame fireworks show, the bulldozer crashed through the wall and rumbled all the way toward home. The highlights of the stadium's demise made ESPN and This Week in Baseball.

The bulldozer that night ended up on top of home plate. Behind it, a pile of dirt sat where the pitcher's mound used to be. A cop car lingered down the right-field line. Auburn players climbed atop the construction equipment, laughing at the absurdity of it all and giving Falcon Park I a not-so-sorrow farewell.

About nine months later, in June 1995, the Auburn Astros opened Falcon Park II in the first of the franchise's back-to-back transformational seasons.

A year later, while maintaining its affiliation with Houston, Auburn ditched the Astros nickname in favor of something more local: the Doubledays. Abner Doubleday, the purported creator of baseball and a Union general during the Civil War, spent part of his childhood in Auburn. His father, Ulysses Doubleday, was a congressman representing Auburn for four years.

The Doubledays work Abners name/likeness into their promoting. The Little Abners Kids Club for children twelve and under grants members free admission to Sunday games and free food while they are there. The Doubledays' mascot and logo is an old-timey baseball player with a mustache that connects to sweet sideburns.

Seeing Double

Auburn and Falcon Park are an awful lot like Batavia and Dwyer Stadium, though the Doubledays haven't quite reached the Muckdogs' levels of existential ambiguity.

It starts with the stadiums themselves. Falcon and Dwyer are nearly identical twins, both built by the same architecture firm (Highland Associates) in the mid-1990s. Both towns are small—though Auburn, with about 27,000 people, has nearly twice as many as Batavia—and both teams are holdovers from when the New York–Penn League was comprised of teams like these in communities like these, before the Brooklyns and the Staten Islands and Connecticuts of the league came to be.

So, yeah, Falcon Park is a bit of a throwback. The box seats—with seat backs and cup

holders—are closest to the field, ten sections stretching across the infield. A walkway separates those from a ring of general-admission bleachers. An overhang protects the GA sections closest to home plate from the elements, with wet and hot extremes both likely at some point over the course of the short season.

Parking is simple and free. Across the street from the third-base side of Falcon Park is a large lot, and beyond the left-field wall is a technically off-site lot that serves as backup.

The neighborhood brings more Auburn-Batavia similarities. Athletic facilities—an ice rink, a pool, tennis and basketball courts—lay beyond the outfield. Casey Park Elementary School is basically next door, which isn't something you see with newer stadiums. Just south of Falcon Park is a residential neighborhood.

Past Greats

Here's a partial look at some noteworthy minor leaguers who played at Falcon Park II before moving on to big league success.

1990s:
Morgan Ensberg, Jason Lane, Julio Lugo, Roy Oswalt, Johan Santana

2000s:
Yan Gomes, Aaron Hill, Brandon League, Adam Lind,

2010s:
Billy Burns, Lucas Giolito, Sandy Leon, Anthony Rendon, Aaron Sanchez

Exceptions to that residential rule are two restaurants, Snapper's Sports Tavern and Sunset, each minutes away by foot. The latter has been family-owned and operated since it opened in 1933.

Falcon Park attendance dipped in 2016 to more than 1,400 fans per game—about half of capacity—which is lower than what the Doubledays drew a decade ago but higher than what they drew three years ago. The team uses special deals to drive attendance on potential/usual slow days: dollar tickets on Mondays, dollar hot dogs on Wednesdays, two-for-one beers on Thursdays.

The Doubledays hired Mike Voutsinas as general manager in 2014, and among his focus areas before leaving after 2016 was a reemphasis on the cleanliness and appearance of the park. "If it looks nice," Voutsinas said. "You'll feel good about going there." That admirable endeavor is—as people who work in the game will tell you—easier to talk about than it is to implement.

The Doubledays replaced the sound system a few years ago, and in 2016 had free WiFi available throughout Falcon Park.

History's Hometown

Abner Doubleday isn't the only famous figure with Auburn connections. The town calls itself "History's Hometown," proud of the role it played during America's early and sometimes dark days.

Noted abolitionists Harriet Tubman and William H. Seward, who also served as secretary of state under Abraham Lincoln and governor of New York, lived in Auburn while helping slaves through the Underground Railroad. Both died in Auburn, too.

Another quirky claim to fame is the Auburn Correctional Facility. A five-minute drive from Falcon Park, it is the oldest continuously operating maximum-security prison in North America. It was constructed in 1816, predating the time Doubleday, Tubman, and Seward spent there.

Ballpark Eats

When Falcon Park II opened in 1995, the team did not anticipate minor league baseball transforming into what it has: an entertainment option complete with food and sideshows, in addition to baseball. And so the team did not anticipate that a lone concession stand would fail to meet demand.

But here the Doubledays are. The stadium's lone food spot is behind home plate, and although Auburn doesn't stray too far from your standard ballpark fare, it does try to offer some variety, including different daily specials—tacos on Tuesdays, for example, and various types of hot dogs (Chicago, St. Louis, nacho) on Wednesdays.

Get To Know a Minor League GM

Jane Rogers, the firecracker of a general manager for the New York–Penn League's Staten Island team, didn't follow a noble calling or true love for the sport like a lot of those in her position did. She worked on Wall Street out of school, then married her husband and had a couple of kids and became a stay-at-home mom.

In 1999, when Rogers was forty-one and looking for work, she saw an ad in the paper. A new minor league team on Staten Island, where she lives, needed an office manager. She applied. She had an interview. She had another. When the team called her in for a final interview, she arrived and met her competition, a woman who was, in Rogers' words, "much younger and had a different look."

When she went in to talk to her future bosses, Rogers—straight shooter—put her hands on her hips and said, "If there's a swimsuit competition, I'm out." They called the next day to offer her the job, as she remembers it.

Going on two decades later, Rogers is running the show in Staten Island, a motherly figure to young ballplayers—some of them teenagers, some of them getting their first real taste of the United States, almost all of them new to New York City—during their summer stay on the island.

"It's almost like they're moving into my house for the summer, and I'm the host," Rogers said.

BATAVIA '98

MUCKDOGS

34 RICKY WILLIAMS   OF

DWYER STADIUM

HOME OF THE
Batavia Muckdogs

LOCATION:	Batavia, NY
TIME FROM:	
ROCHESTER, NY:	45 minutes
BUFFALO, NY:	45 minutes
TORONTO, Canada:	2 hours, 15 minutes
ALBANY, NY:	3 hours, 45 minutes
SCRANTON, PA:	3 hours, 45 minutes
PITTSBURGH, PA:	3 hours, 45 minutes
NEW YORK, NY:	5 hours, 30 minutes
OPENED:	1996
CAPACITY:	2,600
TENANT:	Batavia Muckdogs, Short-Season A New York–Penn League (1996–present)
DISTANCE FROM HOME PLATE:	325 feet to left and right fields, 400 to center
RADIO:	1490 AM and 100.1 FM (Batavia)

Swan song

Dwyer Stadium and the Batavia Muckdogs exist in a purgatorial state, remnants of a minor league world from generations past, holdovers just trying to hold on. As teams move to bigger markets and bigger ballparks, the Muckdogs operate in a general state of up for sale, any season potentially their last. And residents of this tiny upstate New York town know: When professional baseball leaves Batavia, it isn't coming back.

Genesee County Baseball Club owns the Muckdogs. It is an incorporated entity that holds the legal title to the team, with a board of directors of about two dozen people. The Rochester Red Wings operate the team, at a loss, under an agreement with GCBC. Rochester acquires 5 percent of the Muckdogs for every year it runs the Batavia team, capped at 50 percent over 10 years. That deal started in 2007. And so the rumors of the Muckdogs' demise are regular. As soon as a suitor comes along with an offer the Red Wings deem appropriate, the Muckdogs are as good as gone.

Batavia averaged 811 fans per game in 2016. It hasn't done more than 1,000 per since 2011. Other teams in the New York–Penn League to draw that poorly—the Oneonta Tigers, the Jamestown Jammers—moved. It doesn't help, either, that since 2013 the Muckdogs have been affiliated with the Miami Marlins, whose farm system is notoriously shallow.

It wasn't always this way. Dwyer Stadium and Batavia generally have a long hardball history, dating to 1939. That January, in the old Hotel Richmond on Main Street, Batavia served as the birthplace of the Pennsylvania-Ontario-New

York (PONY) League, which years later turned into the modern-day NYPL. Batavia is the lone remaining active founding city.

That same year, Batavia's original stadium opened on the grounds on which Dwyer Stadium stands today. The team renamed the first ballpark after Edward D. Dwyer, the longtime team president, in 1973. The Muckdogs kept the name when the new stadium went up in 1996.

Ready For a Close-up

Dwyer Stadium isn't as old as its throwback feel suggests. Its no-frills, low-key setup lends itself to actually, you know, watching baseball, which isn't always the case in the minor leagues. Dwyer is very similar to Auburn's Falcon Park, designed by the same architects (Highland Associates) and built around the same time (1995 through 1996).

Of Dwyer Stadium's 2,600 seats, about 500 are box seats, spread across ten field-level sections that stretch only as far as just past both dugouts. A walkway separates the box seats

from the general-admission sections, several sets of metal bleachers—a setup that asks for trouble during those hot summer days, but is okay due to usual night games and an overhang that covers much of the seating.

The Muckdogs' only group area is a picnic section down the third-base side, which abuts the home clubhouse/bullpen. There are no suites. Dwyer Stadium has a scoreboard, but no video board.

A plus side to low attendance is that there's no need to worry about traffic or parking. The Muckdogs' on-site lot is free, and fans can park on the street or on an available gravel lot.

Another aspect that sets tiny Dwyer apart from its newer NYPL counterparts: It is one of the few remaining backyard ballparks. Smaller stadiums built in mostly residential areas throughout New York and Pennsylvania used to serve as the backbone of the NYPL, but no longer. Dwyer still fits that profile.

What a Catch

The Batavia Muckdogs get a shout out toward the end of *Summer Catch*, a so-bad-it's-good 2001 baseball movie starring Freddie Prinze Jr. and Jessica Biel. At the end, after Prinze's character completes a summer competing in the famed Cape Cod Baseball League, a Phillies scout approaches with an offer of a professional contract. His first minor league stop? Batavia, New York, home of the Muckdogs.

Beyond the left-field fence are a pair of youth baseball fields. In center, tennis courts. In right, basketball blacktops. Batavia High School, which along with Notre Dame of Batavia gets to play its baseball home games at Dwyer Stadium, is right around the corner. Most of the rest of the immediate neighborhood is houses. Ten minutes and three turns away is Elba, home of those famous mucklands.

Venturing about town, you'll meet a motley crew of major league fans. It's mostly Yankees,

Past Greats

Here's a partial look at some noteworthy big leaguers who played in the new Dwyer Stadium (1998–present).

1990s:

Marlon Byrd, Ryan Madson, Nick Punto, Carlos Silva

2000s:

Matt Adams, Michael Bourn, J.A. Happ, Ryan Howard, Lance Lynn, Chase Utley

2010s:

Kyle Barraclough

Arguably the most famous athlete to play his home games at Dwyer Stadium, a twenty-one-year-old Ricky Williams—yes, the former NFL star running back—saw his pro baseball experiment end in 1998 with the Muckdogs. He hit .283 in thirteen games before returning to the University of Texas and winning the Heisman Trophy as college football's best player.

with a few Mets and Red Sox mixed in, plus Orioles (due to Rochester's former longtime affiliation) and Blue Jays (due to Buffalo's affiliation and Ontario's proximity).

Raining Candy

Batavia is like the minor leagues' minor leagues—what with Triple-A Buffalo and Rochester just forty-five minutes away—and the in-game promotions and gimmicks are fittingly scaled down while maintaining a minor league feel.

Among the goings-on you'll witness is a Chicken Fling, in which one contestant slingshots rubber chickens to another holding a fishing net; a Stars of the Game, in which local youth teams spend time on the field (and in the dugout!) before the game; and your fair share of t-shirt tosses, fireworks nights, and free seat upgrades.

The Muckdogs' signature promotion, though, is something to behold. Once a year, typically on a Sunday afternoon, Batavia organizes a postgame helicopter candy drop, a series of words that should be taken quite literally. Ten minutes after the selected game, a helicopter—owned and flown by a private citizen who volunteers his time and the use of his aircraft—

Ballpark Eats

The Muckdogs' signature concession-stand items are provided by Zweigle's, a Rochester-based meat company. For non-locals, here is a translation for some of the unusual foods, most of which are specific to Western New York.

- **Red hot dog: normal hot dog**
- **White hot dog: pork meat instead of beef (but not a sausage); yes, it is actually white (or close to it)**
- **Muckdog sauce: a hot sauce**
- **Muckdog Chow: a so-called garbage plate—lots of foods piled on top of each other—consisting of red or white hot dog, burger or cheeseburger, homefries, macaroni salad, and Muckdog sauce, all served in a bowl**
- **Also on sale at Dwyer Stadium is off-brand soda and pizza from Ficarella's, a local family-run pizzeria.**

In terms of food options outside the ballpark, Alex's Place—known for its ribs and steaks—is only a five-minute drive down Richmond Avenue. It's at the center of a larger shopping district, which includes a Walmart and BJ's and a horseracing track/casino, Batavia Downs. A couple of minutes in the other direction, Bourbon and Burger offers specialty burgers and a ton of craft beers on tap.

Honoring a Legend

Before the first Dwyer Stadium was known as Dwyer Stadium, it was MacArthur Stadium, christened as such during World War II in honor of General Douglas MacArthur. The stadium name is long gone, but the war hero's name remains on a tiny road between the ballpark and high school: MacArthur Drive.

hovers over Dwyer Stadium, where he dumps 300 pounds of candy onto the field as children eagerly watch. A free-for-all ensues.

That's the sort of quaint—or old-timey or small-town or whatever you want to call it—stuff you'll see in Batavia. Locals host for the summer players from all over the country and world, and most of those players don't have cars or don't bring them to middle-of-nowhere New York. The result? A bunch of young athletic dudes riding around town on bikes mid-June through Labor Day. During games, you can see the players' main mode of transportation lined up in the bullpen.

Who Comes Up with This Stuff?

It's a fair question. Yard Goats and Rumble Ponies and IronPigs and the like—the minor leagues have some weird names, not to mention the off-the-wall logos that come with them.

Increasingly, a tiny San Diego marketing firm can take credit. Brandiose, the brainchild of childhood friends and San Diego natives Jason Klein and Casey White, has worked with about one-third of all minor league baseball teams across the country, including quite a few in the northeast. Yard Goats, Rumble Ponies, IronPigs—that was these guys.

Klein and White were born in the same hospital six days apart and met in kindergarten, but their minor league branding and design story begins during their college days. Closing in on graduation, the pair wrote to 150 minor league teams, offering to redo their logo set. Only one, the West Tenn Diamond Jaxx, responded. Klein and White designed a new logo, and the team bought it. That was more than a decade ago. These days, Brandiose—pronounced like grandi-ose—is a go-to among teams looking to rebrand.

Klein and White have been through enough team rebrandings that they can advise nervous clients on exactly what to expect from their fan base: hesitancy at an announcement, outcry at the likely silly name and logo, then overwhelming acceptance and merchandise sales success.

Giving a baseball team a new identity is a heavy responsibility, and in an effort to get it right—to truly capture a city's personality in the form of a team name and logo—they travel to those cities, talking to locals and getting a sense of what life there is like. That's part of how they picked a scrappy-looking Chihuahua for El Paso and the strong, hardy (Yard) Goats for Hartford.

DODD STADIUM

HOME OF THE
Connecticut Tigers

LOCATION: Norwich, CT

TIME FROM:

HARTFORD, CT: 45 minutes

PROVIDENCE, RI: 1 hour

BOSTON, MA: 1 hour, 45 minutes

MANCHESTER, NH: 2 hours

NEW YORK, NY: 2 hours, 15 minutes

PORTLAND, ME: 3 hours

PHILADELPHIA, PA: 3 hours, 45 minutes

OPENED: 1995

CAPACITY: 6,270

TENANT: Connecticut Tigers, Short-Season A
New York–Penn League (2010–present)

PAST TENANT: Norwich Navigators/Connecticut Defenders,
Double-A Eastern League (1995–2009)

DISTANCE FROM HOME PLATE: 309 feet to left and right fields,
401 feet to center

RADIO: 1310 AM (Norwich)

One Team's Garbage

When the Connecticut Tigers moved into Senator Thomas J. Dodd Memorial Stadium on April 1, 2010, they found a large statue of an anthropomorphic alligator discarded in the woods behind left field. The gator was dressed in full uniform with a baseball bat in hand. It was Tator—Tator the Gator, technically speaking—the mascot for the Norwich Navigators, the Tigers' predecessor. It quickly became the most important piece of garbage in the history of Dodd Stadium.

The Tigers' front-office personnel stashed Tator in the closet for about a year. Then they had him repaired—because sometimes a dude needs a new set of clothes/coat of paint—and during the 2011 season had an unveiling marking Tator's return. The Tigers changed their name to the Navigators for the night in what has since became an annual tradition, and the team put Tator on display in front of Dodd Stadium for all to see.

That statue has turned into a tangible link between two eras of Dodd Stadium baseball. Tator, forever ready for the next pitch, remains outside Dodd's main entrance during the year's more mild months, and it's a popular photo-op spot for families. Children of the 1990s are (gasp) parents themselves now, bringing their kids to see Tator, a remnant of their childhood.

The real Norwich Navigators, who moved to this midsized southeastern Connecticut town and into a brand-new Dodd Stadium as the New York Yankees' Double-A team in 1995, are long gone. They switched their affiliation to the San Francisco Giants in 2003 and their name to the Connecticut Defenders in 2006

before bailing on the northeast completely. In 2010, the Navigators/Defenders became the Richmond Flying Squirrels in Virginia.

Baseball at Dodd Stadium didn't miss a season, though, when the Connecticut Tigers moved in and found the homeless Tator. The Tigers have seen attendance steadily rise through their first few years—from fewer than 1,500 fans per game in 2010 to nearly 2,300 per in 2016—though in a ballpark built for Double-A, there are often plenty of seats to be had.

The Tigers, in a show of commitment to a community that was hesitant after its previous franchise up and left, signed a twenty-five-year lease (technically a ten-year lease with three five-year options) to call Dodd Stadium home for the foreseeable future.

Utility Player

Dodd Stadium has been home to more than just Navigators/Defenders/Tigers baseball in its two-plus decades. Among the extracurriculars:

- ESPN filmed *Bronx is Burning*, its 2007 miniseries about the 1977 New York Yankees, in part at Dodd Stadium
- Bob Dylan/Willie Nelson headlined the same concert at Dodd in June 2005
- The Beach Boys, too, played a concert there, in August 1996
- Various collegiate baseball events—the NEC Tournament, A10 Tournament, a 2010 NCAA Regional hosted by UConn—have been held at Dodd

The stadium is named after Thomas J. Dodd, a politician born in Norwich. He died in 1971. His son, Chris Dodd, served as one of Connecticut's senators for thirty years until 2011.

Have a Seat

Dodd Stadium is a bit oversized for the New York–Penn League, and for the Connecticut Tigers that is a double-edged sword. On, say, gorgeous summer Friday nights, when a sellout or near-sellout crowd comes for a game and fireworks, it's awesome. The more tickets sold, the better. But on slower nights—Mondays, Tuesdays, ugly weather days—Dodd Stadium

What's in a Name?

It is increasingly unusual for a minor league club to share its parent team's name. The Connecticut Tigers (and the not-too-far-away Pawtucket Red Sox) are holdovers from an era in which it was the norm.

The Norwich Navigators and Connecticut Defenders, though, both drew inspiration from a pair of local mainstays. The US Coast Guard Academy is in nearby New London, and Groton is home to a Naval submarine base.

is maybe one-third full, and the atmosphere leaves something to be desired.

The facility, however full, is a nice one. Visitors walk in at street level, and the field is set into the ground. The concourse is closed—an unfortunate reminder that it was built before the open design was commonplace—except toward the ends.

The main bowl is split into three price points. Dugout to dugout includes two of those price

Ballpark Drinks

The Connecticut Tigers and Dodd Stadium take pride in their beer options. And, to be sure, there are many, with a focus on local craft brewers.

- **Hole in the Wall Bar:** Craft beers from all over New England literally come out of holes in the wall behind first base from taps attached to a beer cooler on the other side of the cinder blocks.

- **Retro Beer Bar:** Fancier craft options not your thing? Behind third base, the Tigers offer throwback beers like PBR and Valentine Ale. The previously dormant concession stand also sells pickled sausage and shows *This Week in Baseball* highlights.

- **Southpaws Bar:** It neighbors the large picnic area in the left-field corner and ensures you don't have to walk too far in any direction in order to get your adult beverages.

The Tigers turn Thursday home games into a happy hour of sorts. Gates open early and brewers come to showcase their products.

points, premium box seats closest to the field and reserved seats above those. Down each of the foul lines, there are three sections separated into three price tiers: the first two, plus grandstand seats (metal bleachers).

Grassy berms down the left- and right-field lines, popular among baseball-chasing children, extend to just about the foul poles. The BBQ Pavilion group area down the left-field line is set apart a bit from the field, but includes a deck from which you can watch the game.

At the center of the fifteen-suite upper level is The Yard, a full-service restaurant with outdoor and (air-conditioned!) indoor seating options. It's open to those who buy single-game tickets specific to that area, as well as season-ticket holders and luxury suite ticket holders.

Concessions-wise, Dodd Stadium has two options worth pointing out. Burger Barn, past first base, is a converted old shack that serves specialty burgers, including one named for

Past Greats

Here's a partial look at some noteworthy big leaguers who played at Dodd Stadium over the course of its Double-A and Short-Season A eras.

1990s:

Nick Johnson, Mike Lowell, Eric Milton, Alfonso Soriano, Shane Spencer

2000s:

Madison Bumgarner, Matt Cain, Brandon Crawford, Pablo Sandoval, Marcus Thames, Brian Wilson

2010s:

Devon Travis

The other noteworthy personality with the Tigers in 2016 was hitting coach Mike Hessman, who is something of a minor league legend. Hessman, despite playing in only about 100 major league games in twenty seasons as a pro, is the all-time minor league home run leader with 433. He retired as a player at age thirty-seven after the 2015 season.

former Tigers manager and big leaguer Mike Rabelo (hamburger, spicy sausage, habanero ghost pepper cheese). Down the third-base line is Philly's, a Norwich joint known for their—you guessed it—cheesesteaks.

Dodd Stadium's neighborhood isn't much. Norwich Free Academy, a private school that has produced four big leaguers this century, is around the corner. The plus side to being a bit off the beaten path: Parking is aplenty, and periodic firework nights don't bother anybody.

That part of Connecticut is best known for Mohegan Sun (fifteen minutes from Dodd Stadium) and Foxwoods (thirty minutes away), a pair of resort/casinos.

Loving the Locals

The Tigers' most successful promotions stem from the town/region's background and can be broken down into two categories: Navigators-inspired or locals-inspired.

When the new team came in 2010, it decided to uphold one of the old team's longest traditions: Friday night fireworks, a routine set up by the Navigators in 1995, their first season in town. Those are generally the Tigers' most popular games. Along those lines, the Tigers also host a Norwich Navigators Night every summer, in which they wear jerseys and hats designed after the Navigators' old duds.

Among the locals-inspired promotions is Military Appreciation Night, a typical minor league theme night that means a bit more in Norwich, where the US Coast Guard Academy and Groton's Naval submarine base are so close. The Tigers also started a bobblehead series featuring athletes and famous figures from the area in 2012. That includes former Defenders (Matt Cain, Madison Bumgarner), pro athletes who grew up in or near Norwich (Matt Harvey, Rajai Davis, Matt Shaughnessy), and historical figures (Benedict Arnold, born in Norwich). Arnold's doll was, appropriately, double-sided, with one side dressed like a patriot and the other a redcoat.

Minor League Baseball: A Copycat Business

Here's something worth knowing about minor league baseball: It's a copycat business, and everyone is okay with everyone else stealing their ideas. Teams are more like business partners than competitors, spread out geographically and mostly not really competing to draw the same fans to their ballparks.

That's why you'll see a team one year do a Star Wars Night or a Nickelodeon Night, for example, and then a bunch of other teams host one the next few seasons after that. And someone somewhere along the way had to be first to blast off fireworks after a game, right?

The Lakewood BlueClaws' Ball Brawl game is another good example. In 2015, they introduced the new between-inning contest that involves putting fully grown humans (or nearly fully grown humans) inside giant inflatable balls, then having them run around—usually at each other. The result? Bouncy high-speed collisions.

It was awesome. The game was an immediate hit. At the end of the season, the BlueClaws won a Golden Bobblehead—Minor League Baseball's year-end promotional award—for best on-field promotion.

In 2016, you could find those bouncy, inflatable, human-sized balls at a lot more ballparks.

"The really satisfying part is at end of year," said Greg Giombarrese, the BlueClaws' longtime broadcaster, "when you get calls from other teams who want to do it."

DUTCHESS STADIUM

HOME OF THE
Hudson Valley Renegades

LOCATION: Fishkill, NY

TIME FROM:

NEW YORK, NY: 1 hour, 15 minutes

HARTFORD, CT: 1 hour, 30 minutes

ALBANY, NY: 1 hour, 30 minutes

TRENTON, NJ: 2 hours

PHILADELPHIA, PA: 2 hours, 30 minutes

BOSTON, MA: 3 hours

OPENED: 1994

CAPACITY: 4,494

TENANT: Hudson Valley Renegades, Short-Season A New York–Penn League (1994–present) Manhattan College, NCAA Division I Metro Atlantic Athletic Conference (2015–present)

DISTANCE FROM HOME PLATE: 325 feet to left and right fields, 400 to center

RADIO: 1260 AM (Fishkill) and affiliates

Close Call

The first close call in the history of Dutchess Stadium was not a play on the field. It instead came hours before the first pitch of the first game of the Hudson Valley Renegades' first season, when the gates to The Dutch opened and, well, the place wasn't quite ready for action yet. As fans began to file in, construction crews were said to be bolting in the last few seats and finishing painting the foul poles. The stadium went up in just seventy-one days.

They got it done, though, and fans have shown up in droves ever since. The Renegades perennially average near-sellouts, ranking at or near the top of the New York–Penn League in attendance judged against stadiums' capacities. (The Brooklyn Cyclones, with their 7,000-person MCU Park, regularly lead the league in straight-up gate numbers.)

Many of those fans have had the same question you probably do: What's a Renegade? According to Rick Zolzer, the team's vice president, it's a nod to the Hudson Valley's role in the American Revolution. The region is pockmarked with significant locations of this battle or that encampment. The Americans were renegades of a sort—revolutionists, rebels, traitors to the British crown. One of the finalists in the 1994 name-the-team contest was "Minutemen," which runs along the same theme. In that sense, Renegade fits.

Hudson Valley for a time went with a patriotic red, white, and blue color scheme, but the Revolutionary War motif was never a part of the team's logos or other branding. Instead, they focused on raccoons, a common animal in the area.

More Baseball!

The Renegades play only thirty-eight home games per year (weather pending), which leaves plenty of dates with reasonable baseball conditions. Hudson Valley fills some of those dates with local high school and college teams.

The Manhattan College Jaspers, specifically, started playing their home games at Dutchess Stadium in 2015. The ballpark also hosts an annual contest between Marist (in Poughkeepsie) and Army (the U.S. Military Academy in West Point) the last Wednesday in April.

Dutchess Stadium was also home to the Hudson Valley Fort of the short-lived Fall Experimental Football League in 2015.

Have a Seat

Dutchess Stadium is small and standard, and though there are improvements to be made—financing for the county-owned ballpark is sometimes a point of public consternation and debate—the facility doesn't show its age as much as it does its era.

Built in 1994 to lure the Erie Sailors from their northwestern Pennsylvania home and deteriorating field, The Dutch has a closed concourse and no overhang. The main seating bowl has two sections, split by a walkway, broken up into four price tiers: box, closest to the field; reserved, in the second level behind home plate; reserved grandstand, in the second level behind the dugouts; and general admission, serving as second-level bookends.

There is also one small section of premium boxes down the third-base line.

Dutchess Stadium features three picnic areas. One is behind first base and limited to pre-game use. Then there is one down each of the left- and right-field lines. Neighboring the latter is the "Corona Cantina," which has pub-style seating and high tables. It's open to all fans unless rented out by a group.

The Renegades installed an artificial turf field—rare in the minor leagues—in advance of the 2014 season, in part to avoid issues presented by a poor drainage system. (Remember how crews built Dutchess Stadium in seventy-one days? Apparently they forgot storm drains on the concourse, meaning rainwater ended up on the field.) An ancillary benefit: The Tampa Bay Rays, Hudson Valley's parent team, play on the same type of AstroTurf, so their prospects get a taste of what playing on their major league home field would be like.

Outside The Dutch are four parking lots—or one big lot split into four sections. Whichever way you look at it, with room for 1,200 cars, parking isn't really an issue. What is an issue

is leaving after the game, when everybody is trying to use the same road, Route 9D, to get back to I-84. So just be ready for that and have a little patience.

If it's early enough, hit up Leo's, an Italian joint across the street from the Stadium. Leo's adult children run the show now, and the Renegades have a relationship with the family: A small handful of specialty seats at every home game includes catering from Leo's. They take your order, cook it up, and walk it over mid-game.

What's in a Name?

Dutchess Stadium is another NYPL holdover with a traditional name instead of a branded one. For now, at least, the ballpark gets its name from Dutchess County, the county in which Fishkill sits. The park is sometimes referred to as "The Dutch," which like the county name is a nod to the Dutch people who settled on the land in the late seventeenth century.

Bunch of Rascals

The Renegades are raccoons, don't forget, and the team has slowly built its stable of raccoon mascots since its inception more than twenty years ago. The result is an elaborate and weirdly endearing family history.

Rookie the Renegade was the original. In the second month of the team's first season, he made his move, as recounted in Hudson's Valley official team history: "Rookie the Renegade took a huge chance and asked out Rene Gade, another 6-foot-tall raccoon he met at Dutchess Stadium. They shared their first date July 14."

Those crazy kids dated for two years before Rookie proposed in 1996 "by having a plane circle the stadium with a banner reading 'Rene marry me! –Rookie.'" The answer, of course, was yes, but not before Rene left Rookie on

Ballpark Eats

The Renegades try to add something new to the concessions menu every year, and in 2016 that meant the creation of the Cracker Jack Burger—a cheeseburger with Cracker Jacks stuck on top of the bun with a caramel drizzle. The concoction successfully mixed savory and sweet.

Dutchess Stadium's concessions more generally are broken down into five options. Fortunately, most have straightforward names. You'll find Renegades Pizzeria and Pub, Rascal's Ice Cream, Healthy Hut, Rascal's Sweet Tooth, and Eben's Eatery, which is named after Renegades general manager Eben Yager and serves specialty burgers.

Past Greats

Here's a partial look at some noteworthy big leaguers who played at Dutchess Stadium.

1990s:

Jorge Cantu, Ryan Dempster, Josh Hamilton, Scott Podsednik, Dan Wheeler

2000s:

Wade Davis, Jeremy Hellickson, John Jaso, Evan Longoria, James Shields, Stephen Vogt

Some of those who have played on 2010s Renegades teams will likely become noteworthy in the coming years as the low-level minor leaguers climb up the ladder. Renegades fans tend to know two alumni, Hamilton and Longoria, more than any others. Said one longtime Renegades exec: "After that, it's people giving you side-eyes."

the hook for a couple of innings. They married a season later.

Their child, Rascal, was "born" in 2000. In 2004, Rookie's dad, Roofus, moved in.

That's the sort of goofy, fun-loving stuff you can expect at Dutchess Stadium. In recent years, The Renegades have moved away from giveaways—for whatever reason, bobbleheads and the like aren't big there—but they do mix up the between-inning entertainment (gigantic Hungry Hungry Hippos, anyone?) and have fireworks after every Friday and Saturday home game.

MCU PARK

HOME OF THE
Brooklyn Cyclones

LOCATION:	Brooklyn, NY
TIME FROM:	
QUEENS, NY:	40 minutes
MANHATTAN, NY:	45 minutes
BRONX, NY:	45 minutes
TRENTON, NJ:	1 hour, 15 minutes
PHILADELPHIA, PA:	1 hour, 45 minutes
HARTFORD, CT:	2 hours, 15 minutes
BOSTON, MA:	3 hours, 45 minutes
OPENED:	2001
CAPACITY:	7,000
TENANT:	Brooklyn Cyclones, Short-Season A New York–Penn League (2001–present)
PAST TENANTS:	None
DISTANCE FROM HOME PLATE:	315 feet to left field, 412 to center, 325 to right
RADIO:	90.3 FM (Brooklyn)

Dodgers Connection

Originally known as KeySpan Park, MCU Park went up in the Coney Island neighborhood around the turn of the twenty-first century when New York City brought in two minor league teams—the Brooklyn Cyclones and Staten Island Yankees—to match their big league parents, the Mets and Yankees.

Superstorm Sandy in the fall of 2012 allowed the Cyclones to take their stadium game to the next level. The place was flooded—the dugouts entirely and lowest level of seats partially—and when waters receded the team put in a new artificial turf surface, drainage, and irrigation (salt water ruined the old pipes). That opened the door for more concerts and other events without having to worry about killing or tearing up grass. Among the other events MCU Park has hosted are high school and college baseball, World Baseball Classic qualifiers, professional wrestling, boxing, and semi-pro ultimate Frisbee and football games.

On the field, MCU Park has hosted a pair of New York–Penn League All-Star games (2005 and 2015). The Cyclones have won their division five times—approximately once every three years or so—but have one league title to their credit, named co-champions with the Williamsport Crosscutters in 2001 when the championship series was canceled following the terrorist attacks on September 11.

The history of professional baseball in Brooklyn, of course, extends well beyond the Cyclones' relatively brief existence. An early iteration of the Dodgers called Brooklyn home as early as 1884 right up until their move to Los Angeles in 1957. In a nod to that lengthy history, the Cyclones have a statue of Dodgers legends Jackie Robinson and Pee Wee Reese in front of MCU Park. The team emphasized and embraced that Brooklyn baseball connection early in its existence, but less so in recent years as the Cyclones have developed their own identity.

Mets Reruns

Sterling Equities, led by Fred and Jeff Wilpon, owns the Cyclones as well as the New York Mets, and that connection is clear—especially early in the Cyclones' history. The team's coaching staff has been littered with Mets stars of yesteryear, from an inaugural-season duo of pitching coach Bobby Ojeda and hitting coach Howard Johnson to appearances from Tim Teufel (manager, 2003), Wally Backman (manager, 2010), and Frank Viola (pitching coach, 2011). Edgardo Alfonzo will manage the Cyclones in 2017.

And Baseball, Too

Coney Island was in less-than-great shape before the Cyclones showed up—crime-ridden and generally unattractive—but when MCU Park was built, a more significant police presence and activity in the neighborhood came with it. Billy Harner, who grew up in Brooklyn and works for the Cyclones as director of communications, has watched that evolution. "On a Saturday on the boardwalk," Harner said, "you can't go 20 feet without seeing something that makes you feel safe."

Now, Coney Island is a major tourist destination, and a Cyclones game is just one bullet point on a long list of attractions. There is also the Cyclone wooden roller coaster (from which the team gets its name), the original Nathan's hot dog stand (get a hot dog, of course, but also try the cheese fries bejeweled in bacon bits), and—by the way—the Atlantic Ocean. The view from MCU Park is one of the best in minor league baseball: To the left, the Cyclone and the Wonder Wheel Ferris wheel. To the right, the beach. MCU Park is right off the boardwalk.

If you really want to steer into it, take in a Cyclones game on the Fourth of July, when thousands of tourists flock to Coney Island for Nathan's Hot Dog Eating Contest.

As for the stadium itself, with a maximum capacity of 7,000, MCU Park is among the largest in the league. There is one main level of seating—not protected by any sort of overhang, it's worth noting—plus a ring of luxury boxes. The concourse is open and therefore fan-friendly when it comes to walking and watching.

The only outfield seating is a section of bleachers in right field. It neighbors The Back-

A Word to the Wise

Fair warning before you head into Brooklyn: Traffic is bad, pretty much always. Give yourself plenty of time to get there, especially because there is no shortage of activities on which to spend your spare time. The Cyclones have one decent-size, on-site parking lot, but there is plenty of nearby offsite parking if it's full.

yard in right-center, a hangout area where the view isn't great but the adult beverages (margaritas, beer, wine) and games (shuffleboard, cornhole) are.

Fun, If Not Fundamentals

Many Brooklyn Cyclones players are in their late teens and early twenties, years away from a potential major league debut, and some of them are getting their first taste of professional ball. There are four levels between the Short-Season A NYPL and the big leagues. The quality of play, then, is occasionally understandably sloppy.

Every once in a while, though, you get a Michael Conforto. The Mets' first-round pick in the 2014 MLB draft, Conforto debuted for the Cyclones that summer, getting his start in the NYPL like lots of other top-notch college players. Conforto dominated. Fourteen months later, he was hitting home runs—yes, plural—in the World Series for the Mets. The lesson? The majors are several miles and a world away for the young Cyclones, but sometimes you see something and someone special anyway.

The Cyclones deviate from baseball norms—while embracing the neighborhood feel—by deploying a cheering squad known endearingly as the Beach Bums, who regularly perform dance routines, assist with in-game promotions, and are a general meet-and-greet, face-of-the-Cyclones presence.

The carnival-like atmosphere that envelops Coney Island during summer nights infiltrates MCU Park on Fridays, when fireworks blast off from the beach at 9:30 p.m.—even if the Cyclones are still playing. (Fireworks can be held

Throwbacks Catch On

When Harner & Co. wanted to put on a Nickelodeon Night—complete with Kel Mitchell of Kenan & Kel fame, green slime, and a makeshift Double Dare course—the Cyclones called the kids-centric cable channel. Nickelodeon was into it. It was such a success that Nickelodeon brought similar promotions to other minor league teams, and by 2016 it evolved into what was essentially a countrywide tour of mostly minor league stadiums.

until 9:59 p.m. if the game is close to finishing, but no later.) The brightly colored explosives are visible from MCU and are right in the batter's line of vision. The Cyclones explain the situation to umpires and visiting teams beforehand, and all parties are usually fine with it. They haven't stopped a game for it in almost a decade.

A Promotion About Nothing

Here's a scene straight out of a minor league fever dream for you: Middle of the summer, a hot Sunday afternoon, bottom of the ninth, the home team down by more than two touchdowns . . . and the stands utterly packed, every one of the 8,241 in attendance willingly sticking around to and through the end of the game.

Billy Harner, the Brooklyn Cyclones' PR guru, couldn't believe what he was seeing at MCU Park on July 5, 2014. But it was very, very real. The team's Salute to *Seinfeld* Night—a themed day at the ballpark in honor of the twenty-fifth anniversary of the "show about nothing"—was wildly successful.

"Nobody left. It was like a perfect explanation of what minor league baseball is. People don't necessarily come for the actual game," Harner said. "For us to have a game where we lost 18 to 2, but nobody leaves and everybody is talking about how much fun they had even though the home team lost by that many runs, that makes us all feel good because it means we're doing our job."

Harner and the rest of the Cyclones' marketing/promotions staff indeed do their jobs, and they do them well—better than any other minor league team in the country, perhaps. That initial *Seinfeld* Night was the most successful venture, garnering about $8 million worth of publicity and drawing fans from at least twenty-six states and five countries, but the Cyclones periodically make headlines and win awards with their themed days and promotions.

Seinfeld Night in 2014 earned the Cyclones a Golden Bobblehead, Minor League Baseball's annual best-of marketing awards, for best theme night, and with reason. The list of gimmicks, giveaways, and contests based around *Seinfeld* jokes (some of them obscure) ran deep. A man named George Costanza drove down from Rhode Island to throw out the first pitch. The first 3,000 fans to show up received a Keith Hernandez Magic Loogie bobblehead. The Cyclones took batting practice in puffy shirts. There was a Dance Like Elaine contest and a low-talking PA announcer. Fans were allowed to run around the bases—a typical minor league happening—and anybody named Jerry got a head start. Larry "Soup Nazi" Thomas brought his cart and sold real soup, the line dozens deep.

Harner's favorite part, however, was a pregame Snickers-eating contest in which participants had to use a knife and fork. It was hot out, and the chocolate was messy. An hour before the game, the crowd was going nuts, watching a handful of regular people eat candy with utensils.

"I looked around and thought, This is the most absurd thing," Harner recalled with a laugh. "It was a moment I sat back and realized what we had done."

Seinfeld Night returned to MCU Park in 2015 (featuring a Little Jerry bobblehead and a muffin top–popping contest) and again 2016, a "*Seinfeld* fan's *Seinfeld* Night," as Harner put it, the deep well of jokes starting to run dry. Still, the Cyclones brought in John O'Hurley (the actor who played J. Peterman), gave away Roger McDowell Second Spitter bobbleheads, and had an envelope-licking contest (in which nobody died!). The tagline? "Make Kramerica Great Again."

It was all a bit of a passion project for Harner, a Brooklyn native and hardcore *Seinfeld* fan who visited *Seinfeld* trivia nights to pick the brains of like-minded folks.

"He's the mastermind behind that," said Cyclones GM Kevin Mahoney. "I'm pretty sure he knows every episode by heart."

The Cyclones' high-profile theme nights extend beyond *Seinfeld*, but there is a certain force driving it all: nostalgia. Specifically, '90s nostalgia. In 2015, the team put on Salute to *Saved by the Bell* Night. In 2016 it was *Full House* and later a Jimmy Fallon Night. For that last one, a project three years in the making, the Cyclones slow-jammed the lineups and had an Everybody's Talking Bout My Tight Pants race.

The Brooklyn staff doesn't limit the creativity to Cyclones games. The team's other recent Golden Bobblehead was for best non–game day event, Ambush Baseball. For that one, the club colluded with parents and

Ballpark Eats

Here's the thing about the modern-day minor league arms race: Fans are a tad spoiled! That's increasingly true when it comes to concessions. "It's more than just hot dogs and hamburgers," as one Cyclones employee put it. "That's what people have come to expect."

At MCU Park, the Cyclones have made a concerted effort to inject a true taste of Brooklyn into the food options, including Grandma's House, on the third-base concourse. We suggest the chopped steak sandwich. Or try Arancini Bros, behind home plate, for a variety of rice balls (including Nutella and mac and cheese).

Past Greats

Here's a partial look at some noteworthy big leaguers who played at MCU Park in Brooklyn on their way to the majors.

2000s:

Scott Kazmir, Angel Pagan, Brian Bannister, Bobby Parnell, Daniel Murphy, Ike Davis, Dillon Gee, Lucas Duda, Juan Lagares, Wilmer Flores

2010s:

Michael Conforto

coaches of a local Little League team to show up at a field, tell the kids their game was canceled, and transport them all to MCU Park for an impromptu game at the pros' place.

"Many teams do so many great things, so to be considered among the best is an honor," Harner said.

So that's what you're getting and who you're dealing with when you go to a Cyclones game. If you want to go to a game, maybe take a gander at the promotional schedule before you pick which one. The Cyclones probably have something up their (puffy) sleeve.

"Minor league baseball as an industry is filled with the most creative people in the world," Harner said. "If any of us had half a brain, we'd be making a lot more money doing something else."

RICHMOND COUNTY BANK BALLPARK

HOME OF THE
Staten Island Yankees

LOCATION: Staten Island, NY

TIME FROM:

MANHATTAN, NY: 45 minutes

QUEENS, NY: 45 minutes

BROOKLYN, NY: 45 minutes

BRONX, NY: 1 hour

TRENTON, NJ: 1 hour, 15 minutes

PHILADELPHIA, PA: 1 hour, 45 minutes

HARTFORD, CT: 2 hours, 30 minutes

OPENED: 2001

CAPACITY: 7,171

TENANT: Staten Island Yankees, Short-Season A New York–Penn League (2001–present)

Wagner College baseball (2008–present)

PAST TENANTS: None

DISTANCE FROM HOME PLATE: 320 feet to left field, 390 to center, 318 to right

RADIO: 88.9 FM (Staten Island)

Babies No More?

The Staten Island Yankees, the New York–Penn League twin of the Brooklyn Cyclones, are actually two years older than their home Richmond County Bank Ballpark, playing their first pair of seasons at the College of Staten Island. When RCB Ballpark opened in 2001, the Yankees moved in.

Since then, the so-called Baby Bombers—a play on the New York Yankees' Bronx Bombers nickname—have periodically dominated the NYPL, winning the league title six times and their division eight times. The Yanks get a bad rap for mostly not developing homegrown tal-

Ahead of Its Time

St. George, the team's neighborhood within the borough of Staten Island, was actually the former site of the St. George Stadium, home of the New York Metropolitans (1886–86) and New York Giants (1889). In a the-more-things-change sense, St. George Stadium was well ahead of its time, complete with dining rooms that allowed fans to eat and watch baseball simultaneously and an offseason slate of theater functions (and sometimes a circus). Wrote The *New York Times* in April 1886, after the Metropolitans' first game: "The grand stand overlooks the bay, and a cool, refreshing breeze adds to the comfort of the onlookers; the playing grounds are neatly sodded, and altogether the Metropolitans can boast of one of the best parks in the country."

ent in the early parts of the twenty-first century, but that seemingly hasn't limited their Short-Season A affiliate.

The next time Staten Island wins the New York–Penn League, its jerseys might not say "Yankees." The team decided in 2016 to rebrand and change its name, but coming up with the right identity has been a challenge. The change was tabled heading in the 2017 season but remains a possibility for future years. The eventual goal is to give local residents something more borough-specific to hang on to and embrace. "We are very proud to be Yankees," team president Will Smith said when the team made the announcement, "but equally proud to be part of this community."

The NYPL, it seems, loves New York. RCB Ballpark hosted the All-Star Game in 2010, and when you factor in Brooklyn hosting the 2005 and 2015 editions, the league seems to be on an every-five-years mid-summer visit to the Big Apple. So keep an eye out come 2020.

Changing Views

Richmond County Bank Ballpark, more than a decade and a half old, still feels fresh and clean and easy to navigate. The façade is sharp, and when you walk in through the main gates you look down at the playing field, set below street level. The stadium was designed this way to take advantage of the gorgeous view beyond the outfield fence. From left to right, you can see the skylines of Jersey City (New Jersey), Manhattan, and Brooklyn—plus the Hudson River and the Statue of Liberty. Several times a game, gigantic cargo ships pass by, momentarily impeding that view while providing a new one.

RCB Ballpark has one seating bowl, which is divided into three price points, increasingly expensive (but never very expensive) the closer you get to home plate. A second level is full of suites for group outings and an open section behind home plate—protected by netting, to be sure—where the team hosts an all-you-can-eat buffet for interested parties.

The concourse between the levels is open but narrow, opening the door for congestion on days with large crowds. Down the right-field line, there is a picnic deck that offers tables with umbrellas, but RCB lacks large party areas and outfield seating in fair territory.

The stadium really does abut the Hudson, the two separated by only a narrow paved road. With water on one side and a road on the other—and a 9/11 memorial and park mixed in—the club is limited as far as potential physical expansions go.

Parking was effectively nonexistent for much of 2016, but the newly constructed garage well beyond left field should ease that situation. This is especially important given Staten Island's largely suburban feel and the many cars that come with it.

As far as the larger neighborhood goes, it's not great. But you can pick your spots to venture out into if you know enough and have a specific destination. The original Ralph's Italian Ices shop isn't far, and there are three nice "B" restaurants—Blue (American/Mediterranean), Beso (Spanish tapas), and Bayou (New Orleans Cajun)—within walking distance.

Plenty of Potential

The Staten Island Yankees, even in their brief history, boast quite a few major league alums—including potential future Hall of Famer Robinson Cano—underscoring the idea that the Yankees' stars of tomorrow are in Staten Island today. And, in following in their parent team's footsteps, the club has retired quite a few numbers already: Number 6 (Brett Gardner), Number 17 (Cano), Number 19 (Jason Anderson), and Number 41 (Chien-Ming Wang).

To that effect, Staten Island has traditionally been a safe bet to be a fun, exciting team, regularly contending for division and league titles. That's not always the case for minor league teams, where the year-to-year player turnover is close to 100 percent. If nothing else, the Yankees' early-round draft picks usually come with a certain degree of hype and expectation, so they are worth checking out each summer, too.

Hot Dogging It

Concessions-wise, RCB Ballpark offers mostly your standard fare, but with a bit of a twist when it comes to hot dogs. Every offseason, the team invites fans to submit recipes for a new specialty hot dog to be sold at games. The front office passes those recipe ideas by the folks who run the kitchen, and they pick finalists. Fans vote online for the winner, and the results can be . . . interesting. The McNamara Dog, for example, won in 2014. The dog was topped with baked beans, bacon, sour cream, cheddar, and mustard.

Staten Island does a good job with its promotional schedule, going above and beyond your usual fireworks night here and team-branded swag there. Peruse the 2016 slate for evidence: Sabermetrics Day, Star Wars Night (including an Evil Empire hat giveaway), eSports Night, and Pat Venditte Bobblehead giveaway day (in honor of the ambidextrous pitcher and former SI Yank).

Oh, and did you know Staten Island is in New York? If the view of the Manhattan skyline isn't enough, the PA system blasts Big Apple–themed songs, from Frank Sinatra to Taylor Swift to Jay-Z.

Destination St. George

The Staten Island Yankees, for the entirety of their existence, have been a bit of a paradox.

Yes, they're in New York City—but Staten Island isn't really New York City. It is set aside geographically from its Manhattan, Brooklyn, Queens, and Bronx siblings, and, hell, the people there even wanted to secede as recently as the 1990s. It is endearingly called the Forgotten Borough.

And yes, the Yankees are the Yankees—but they're not really the Yankees. They're the minor league Yankees, part of a feeder system for the major league Yankees, the twenty-seven-time World Series champions and perhaps the most recognizable sports-team brand in the world. The Staten Island Yankees are, if you will, the forgotten Yankees.

So Staten Island, borough and team, has endured an identity crises of sorts for most of this century. And Staten Island, borough and team, is working to change that. That effort is happening simultaneously on two fronts: the Destination St. George campaign, a $1.2 billion investment in the neighborhood at the northern tip of Staten Island, and the Staten Island Yankees' impending rebrand and name change, originally scheduled for 2017 but delayed indefinitely when the team couldn't settle on the right new name after the 2016 season.

First, Staten Island the borough.

John Bruno, as proud a New Yorker and Yankee fan as you'll find, isn't quite a lifelong Staten Island resident. You'll have to excuse the year and a half shortly after World War II when Bruno was an infant and his family lived

Past Greats

Here's a partial look at some noteworthy big leaguers who played in Staten Island on their way to the majors.

2000s:

Dellin Betances, Robinson Cano, Melky Cabrera, Francisco Cervelli, Phil Coke, Michael Dunn, Brett Gardner, Ian Kennedy, Mark Melancon, David Phelps, Chien-Ming Wang

2010s:

Gary Sanchez

Leftover Yankees

The Staten Island Yankees, jumping aboard the revitalization train (or ferry), will play under a new name eventually. There is nothing wrong with the Yankees moniker, and in the franchise's early days it helped establish some legitimacy. But the shine has worn off.

Just ask—again—John Bruno. He grew up visiting Yankee Stadium with his dad in the days of Mickey Mantle, Yogi Berra, and Whitey Ford. When he got a little older, he took the subway on his own. A little older than that, he drove. The constant through the years, in addition to living on Staten Island, was Yankees baseball.

When the Yankees partnered up with a minor league team to bring an affiliate to Staten Island—Bruno's Staten Island—he was quite literally the first person in line for tickets. After he waited overnight in a strip mall parking lot in March 1999, team employees called him their number one fan and he made the front page of the local paper, the *Staten Island Advance*.

By the end of 2016, Bruno hadn't been to a game in a season and a half. In choosing a new team, something special to Staten Island that the community can embrace, the team hopes to inject some energy into what should be a built-in fan base on the Island.

"This community that we're a part of doesn't get a chance to have its own identity through its team. Everywhere you go, people wear sports logos [to signify where they're from]. You can't do that for Staten Island," said a front-office staffer. "They always get the leftovers. It sucks to be the leftover Yankees, too.

"It's part of being a component of the general improvement of life here, having a cultural icon that belongs to this borough—as opposed to an offshoot of bigger, better things."

elsewhere, plus the handful of months when he moved to Florida because his wife thought it would be great. (It wasn't. It was too hot, and they moved back.)

So take Bruno's word for it when he says Staten Island is the runt of the New York City litter. "We're the last to get anything," he says. "If we do get anything." Among the issues: high tolls, poor public transportation, slowly re-paved roads, lack of relief after Superstorm Sandy. Perceived or real, the slights Staten Islanders see are not forgotten, even if the dynamic has improved in recent years. "People would treat Staten Island as a dumping ground,"

Bruno says. "In fact, we had the biggest dump in the world." He's not kidding: The Fresh Kills Landfill, which closed around the turn of the twenty-first century, once held that title.

To do away with its Forgotten Borough reputation, Staten Island is trying to become a hotspot. It is spelling out that desire in plain language via its Destination St. George campaign, whose official website bills the area as "New York City's next waterfront destination."

The idea is simple: Draw people to St. George, the neighborhood on the North Shore that includes the Yankees' RCB Ballpark. For years, that has been nearly impossible. The only draw is the Staten Island Ferry, which is free and runs between Manhattan and St. George, and the Staten Island Yankees, who play thirty-eight home games per year.

"They get off the ferry, swing around and go back," says Jane Rogers, the baseball team's general manager. "Tourists come here around noon, they're not even sure what this [ballpark] is. They're peering through the gates. We have to be able to capture that when it happens."

The solution: If you build it, they will come. The "it," in this case, is a variety of attractions. Empire Outlets will be an upscale shopping center. The New York Wheel will be the biggest Ferris wheel in the world, a thirty-eight-minute ride for hundreds of people at a time. Mix in a few existing options—including a baseball game, the Staten Island Museum, and St. George Theatre—and there is easily a day's worth of activities for would-be visitors. Folks at RCB Ballpark are, as you can imagine, excited about what the future might hold.

"It should be really good for us, and it should be really good for the community," says one team employee. "It's only going to help us. It should help us a lot."

BB&T BALLPARK AT HISTORIC BOWMAN FIELD

HOME OF THE
Williamsport Crosscutters

LOCATION: Williamsport, PA

TIME FROM:

HARRISBURG, PA:	1 hour, 45 minutes
SCRANTON, PA:	1 hour, 45 minutes
BALTIMORE, MD:	3 hours
PHILADELPHIA, PA:	3 hours
NEW YORK, NY:	3 hours, 15 minutes
PITTSBURGH, PA:	3 hours, 15 minutes

OPENED: 1926

CAPACITY: 4,200

TENANT: Williamsport Crosscutters, Short-Season A New-York Penn League (1994–present)

PAST TENANTS:

Williamsport Bills, Double-A Eastern League (1987-91)

Williamsport Tomahawks, Double-A Eastern League (1976)

Williamsport Astros/Red Sox, Short-Season A New York–Penn League (1968-72)

Williamsport Mets, Double-A Eastern League (1964-67)

Williamsport Grays, various names/leagues (1926-1962)

Eight others

DISTANCE FROM HOME PLATE: 345 feet to left field, 405 to center, 350 to right

RADIO: 1050 AM and 104.1 FM (Williamsport)

Emphasis on "Historic"

You have heard of Williamsport before—about every August, say—but probably not in the context of professional baseball. Williamsport is best known as home of the Little League World Series, the annual international baseball tournament for eleven- to thirteen-year-olds.

But just a seven-minute drive away from the LLWS complex, right on the other side of the Susquehanna River, is BB&T Ballpark at Historic Bowman Field, home of the Williamsport Crosscutters and many teams before them.

Built for just $75,000 in the Roaring Twenties, the stadium originally known as Bowman Field has seen generations of fans, a whole lot of baseball, and periodic renovations through the decades. During those alterations—lights in 1932, a concrete base for box seats in 1947, auditorium-style chairs replacing wooden ones in 1987, new clubhouses in 1994—Williamsport

Pedal to the Metal

Williamsport is close geographically to nothing, but about three hours from a bunch of major east-coast cities—Philly and Pittsburgh, New York and Baltimore (and then D.C.)—so Williamsportians are used to making that six-hour round trip in a day for a big-time sporting event, which has resulted in murky major league allegiances. The Phillies have a slight edge over the Pirates baseball-wise, with at least three other teams about as far as those two, and football fandom is even less clear.

Let There Be Light

A fun footnote to Bowman Field's long history: In 1964, the Williamsport club was affiliated with the New York Mets, who had just moved into the brand-new Shea Stadium. That left their temporary home, the Polo Grounds, empty and soon demolished. The Mets sent Williamsport the Polo Grounds' lights, which illuminated Bowman Field for more than two decades.

has worked to maintain the traditional feel of Bowman Field, allowing it to continue to blend into a historic neighborhood while providing some modern-day experiences.

Williamsport was like a lot of minor league towns in the early days of minor league baseball, enduring regular change of teams and names every few years, but the later parts of the twentieth century brought a degree of stability. In 1994, the Geneva Cubs moved to Williamsport to become the Williamsport Cubs, a short-season team that brought baseball back to Bowman Field after a two-year layoff.

When the club's affiliation switched to Pittsburgh in 1999 (and then again to Philadelphia in 2006), the team changed its name to the Crosscutters, a nod to the town's former status as the Lumber Capital of the World.

What's in a Name?

Williamsport's ballpark is a case study in the modernization of stadium names. Originally and briefly dubbed Memorial Field, from 1929

until 2000 it was called Bowman Field, after J. Walton Bowman, a local figure significant in bringing baseball to town in the 1920s. In 2000, the name changed to Historic Bowman Field and stayed that way until 2014. From 2014 to 2015 it was known as Susquehanna Bank Park at Historic Bowman Field. In 2016 it changed to its current moniker of BB&T Ballpark at Historic Bowman Field when BB&T bought out Susquehanna Bank, a transaction almost certainly worth it solely because the stadium's name became a slightly smaller mouthful.

A Baseball Capital

In modern minor league baseball, ballparks worth experiencing tend to fall into two general categories: gorgeous and new and shiny,

or older and traditional and quaint. And, to be sure, it's worth trying both.

BB&T Ballpark at Historic Bowman Field falls into the latter grouping. A throwback nearly a century old, it is not especially fancy and won't wow you with a gigantic video board—or any video board—or other electronic distractions. The closed concourse is limited to behind home plate, closer to a large rectangle than the more typical long hallway.

BB&T Ballpark, like some of its fellow elderly NYPL brethren, has some quirks to it. Most notably, the dugouts are farther down the foul lines than normal, lined up with the outer edge of the infield dirt and the start of the outfield grass.

Between the inside ends of the dugout—more or less from third base to first base—is the only reserved seating in the stadium, seven-row sections of individual seats. Beyond that, the rest of the main bowl is a general admission Family Section, which might give way to new individual seats in the coming years.

Bordered by Lycoming Creek on one side and Blaine Street on another, BB&T Ballpark doesn't have much room for potential expansion, and there is no outfield seating. The Crosscutters' options for improvements are to build up—which is difficult and rather expensive—or renovate what they have. They have gone with renovations of late.

Down the third-base line, the team has made moves in recent years to offer some modern amenities, including the Cutter's Cove picnic spot for groups and a fifty-person Dugout Deck behind the visitors' dugout. The deck has high-top tables and chairs and is said to be rather popular. Down the first-field line, the Crosscutters removed a set of uncovered bleachers in favor of a multi-tier premium deck, the latest in a series of $1.2 million renovations.

The ballpark, owned by the city, sits in Memorial Park, which includes a swimming pool, playground, and a couple of picnic areas. There is a parking lot for about 100 cars on-site, but other than that it's a wherever-you-can-fit situation. Beyond the park, the neighborhood is largely residential, including Millionaires' Row along West Fourth Street. Williamsport, once the lumber capital of the world, for one stretch in the late 1800s had more millionaires per capita than any city in the country. Their big old homes are now a historic district with walking tours, right near BB&T Ballpark.

Williamsport is a sneaky-awesome baseball destination. Affiliated minor league ball is a good start, and in addition to the Little League World Series in August, you can also visit the first-ever Little League field, Original Field, right in Memorial Park. A half-hour down US-15 in Lewisburg is the gravesite of Christy Mathewson, an all-time great pitcher from the early twentieth century and a member of the Hall of Fame's first class (1936).

Ballpark Eats

The Crosscutters don't stray much from your standard ballpark fare, though there seems to be a focus on barbecue items—including pulled pork and brisket from Acme Barbecue, a popular local joint only a few minutes away by car.

If you're looking for another taste-of-town type of eatery, Park Pizza—established in 1960!—is right behind the ballpark on Memorial Avenue. Pizza, wings, and Stromboli dominate the menu, so it has pretty much anything you really need.

The Great Potato Caper

Dave Bresnahan was a light-hitting catcher/first baseman from Arizona who played a handful of minor league seasons in the 1980s, including 1987 with the Double-A Williamsport Bills, a Cleveland Indians affiliate. And with one goofy play, Bresnahan forever etched his name in baseball lore.

Bresnahan decided to put his prank, weeks in the making, into action on August 31, 1987. The Williamsport Bills were playing the Reading Phillies at Bowman Field. There were two outs in the top of the fifth inning; Reading's Rick Lundblade was on third base.

After a low pitch, Bresnahan fired toward third base—a routine play, trying to catch the runner straying too far from the base—but the "ball" went down the line into left field. Lundblade skipped home, only to be greeted by Bresnahan, ball in hand and smile on his face. Bresnahan had thrown a potato, molded to look like a baseball, to fool Lundblade on a trick play. The sequence has been dubbed The Great Potato Caper.

Umpires called Lundblade safe. The Indians cut Bresnahan the next day. He never played pro ball again, eventually turning to a career in real estate in Arizona. The actual potato Bresnahan threw is preserved in denatured alcohol and on display at The Baseball Reliquary, a non-profit educational organization in Pasadena, California.

In 1988, the year after the prank, Williamsport held a Dave Bresnahan Day and retired his Number 59. He visits every few years and is the subject of many articles recounting his exploits. In 2012, the Crosscutters put Bresnahan in the Bowman Field Hall of Fame.

Past Greats

Here's a partial look at some noteworthy big leaguers who played at BB&T Ballpark for Williamsport's most recent franchise, which was known as the Cubs from 1994-98 before adopting the Crosscutters name.

1990s:
Eric Hinske, Kerry Wood

2000s:
Jose Bautista, Matt Capps, Travis d'Arnaud, Rajai Davis, Andrew McCutchen, Jonathan Villar, Neil Walker

2010s:
Maikel Franco

A handful of Hall of Famers played for previous Williamsport teams, including Jim Bunning, Bill Mazeroski, Nolan Ryan, and Jim Rice.

MEDLAR FIELD AT LUBRANO PARK

HOME OF THE
State College Spikes

LOCATION:	State College, PA
TIME FROM:	
HARRISBURG, PA:	1 hour, 30 minutes
SCRANTON, PA:	2 hours, 15 minutes
PITTSBURGH, PA:	2 hours, 30 minutes
BALTIMORE, MD:	2 hours, 45 minutes
PHILADELPHIA, PA:	3 hours, 15 minutes
NEW YORK, NY:	3 hours, 45 minutes
OPENED:	2006
CAPACITY:	5,570
TENANTS:	State College Spikes, Short-Season A New York–Penn League (2006–present) Pennsylvania State University baseball, NCAA Division 1 (2006–present)
PAST TENANTS:	None
DISTANCE FROM HOME PLATE:	325 feet to left field, 399 to center, 320 to right
RADIO:	1390 AM (State College)

We Are

The New York–Penn League has engaged in a stadium/facility arms race of sorts this century—with Brooklyn and Staten Island building nice new parks and Connecticut moving into a previously built large one, among other machinations—and the State College Spikes kept pace by joining forces with Pennsylvania State University.

In 2005, Penn State built Medlar Field at Lubrano Park, named after Charles "Chuck" Medlar, a former longtime baseball coach at the

This Really Happened

Medlar Field bore witness to a hilariously only-in-the-minors occurrence one night in August 2016: a goat delay. There is no typo there. A goat snuck onto the field and forced a game between the State College Spikes and Batavia Muckdogs to stop for about a minute and a half.

How did it happen? When the Spikes' mascot ran onto the field during a celebratory moment, the goat—in town with the Cowboy Monkey Rodeo, a traveling act in which a monkey riding a sheepdog herds the goat and his or her friends—jaunted through the momentarily open door. Players gawked as seven members of the grounds crew corralled the animal and more or less dragged it off the field.

"You won't see this at Fenway," said the utterly jubilant play-by-play man that night. "There's a goat on the field stopping the game! Or a sheep! Or whatever!"

school, and Anthony P. Lubrano, a Penn State alumnus whose $2.5 million donation helped bring the park into existence. Around the same time, the Spikes' new owners moved them from New Jersey to central Pennsylvania. The ensuing partnership was a natural one and has proven to be mutually beneficial.

Penn State owns the ballpark. The Spikes operate it year-round. Penn State plays its home schedule mid-March through mid-May, plus or minus a week, and the Spikes play mid-June through early September. Each team has its own clubhouse (in part due to NCAA amateurism rules) in addition to a third for visiting

Pittsburgh Lookalike

The dimensions of Medlar Field are identical to that of PNC Park—the home of the Pittsburgh Pirates, State College's former parent team—with one fun exception. The right-field wall in Pittsburgh is 21 feet high in honor of Hall of Famer Roberto Clemente. At State College, the right-field wall is 18.55 feet high in honor of the year of Penn State's founding, 1855.

teams. Both programs have office space in the building.

The result for State College? One of the nicer stadiums in short-season ball. The setup is similar to what the Vermont Lake Monsters had with the University of Vermont (which has since cut its baseball program), except in this case Penn State is a big-time athletics school. That means a nice facility right off the bat and plenty of funds for regular maintenance.

The unusual relationship extends beyond baseball season, too. The Spikes gave away a bobblehead of former Penn State quarterback Christian Hackenberg, for example, and during

Penn State fall football home games—almost always on Saturdays after Spikes season is over—Medlar Field suites are available for rent for tailgating goings-on. The ballpark is adjacent to Beaver Stadium. The fine print of that availability, via the Spikes' website, offers a hint at the often-jovial college football tailgating culture: "Access to the suite level begins at 8 a.m."

Sit Like a King

Medlar Field's main seating bowl is one level with three different price points based on closeness to home plate. Behind the backstop is the Diamond Club, bookended by the field box seats, which more or less align with third and first base. Farther down the foul lines are the Bullpen Box seats. A second level is full of luxury suites.

Ballpark Eats

The Spikes brand most of their concession stands, oftentimes partnering with local eateries. You'll find barbecue down the third-base line and gourmet burgers in right, plus other specialty stands—including one for just dessert. Among the nearby businesses in on the action are Bradley's Cheesesteaks & Hoagies, Rosie's Pierogies, Ye Olde College Diner (known for its sticky buns), Penn State Berkey Creamery (ice cream), and many local breweries (there are eight different beers available at Medlar).

What's in a Name?

As with any respectable minor league team name, Spikes is a double entendre. Spikes is another word for cleats, the shoes baseball players wear, as well as a reference to deer, a common animal in the region. A young deer's budding antler—an easy symbol for a young ballplayer's budding career—is called a "spike."

Unlike most NYPL parks, Medlar Field has some outfield seating. Left field features the Pepsi Picnic Pavilion, where groups of twenty or more can enjoy an all-you-can-eat-buffet. That neighbors the Kids' Zone of inflatables and games and a Wiffle ball field (on a miniature Medlar Field!). Across the way in right are a couple of bleacher sections as well as Rail Kings deck seats, which comes with waitress/waiter service and personal TVs. The Spikes' Fun Deck, also in the right-field corner, is a patio area.

The entire stadium is set near the foot of Mount Nittany, which creates quite the view beyond the outfield fence.

If Medlar Field sharing space with Penn State—a large state university with the reputation of being a party school—gives you pause, fear not. The Spikes play in the summer, when most of the college kids are gone and State College has more of a laid-back, low-key feel to it.

To that effect, parking is aplenty at Medlar Field. Lot 44—situated between Medlar Field, Beaver Stadium, and the Bryce Jordan Center—is gigantic, certainly enough for a Spikes game. Penn State football and basketball, which play in the same athletic complex, draw many more thousands of fans (at different times of the year) and use the same lots.

A Favorite Fan

The Spikes engage in your typical minor league promotions—plenty of fireworks, Bark in the Park dog days, Military Appreciation Night—but their most popular giveaway and themed night has nothing to do with any of that.

In July 2016, the Spikes hosted Strike Out Progeria Night in honor of Josiah Viera, an inspirational little boy whose story can't be done justice in a couple of hundred words here. Go ahead and Google it (and then come read the rest of this book).

Josiah has Progeria, a rare and incurable genetic disorder sometimes called Benjamin Button Disease that accelerates aging. Josiah also loves—loves—baseball. With the Children's Miracle Network in 2013, a then-nine-year-old Josiah made what was supposed to be a one-time visit to State College and a Spikes game.

Pitcher Mitch Harris—who also has a fascinating story, pursuing professional baseball and reaching the major leagues in 2015 after serving five years in the Navy—and other members of that year's Spikes team struck up a friendship with Josiah, who returned repeatedly over the course of that season. He has become a regular presence at Medlar Field in the summers since, and the St. Louis Cardinals, the Spikes' parent team, have hosted Josiah at spring training on multiple occasions.

And so one summer night at Lubrano Park, the Spikes had a night dedicated to raising

Past Greats

Here's a partial look at some noteworthy big leaguers who played at Medlar Field in its brief history.

2000s:
Allen Craig, Luke Gregerson, Brock Holt, Jason Motte, Adam Ottavino, Tony Watson

2010s:
Josh Bell, Tyler Glasnow, Mitch Harris, Dilson Herrera, Gregory Polanco

The Spikes honor their major league alumni by hanging their photos on the concourse behind home plate.

awareness of Progeria and money to research it. Josiah was the star. The first 1,000 fans through the gates received a Josiah Viera bobblehead. The Spikes made Josiah their honorary bench coach. He hung around batting practice and wore his own uniform. He, being among the savviest preteens you'll meet, tipped his cap to the adoring crowd. He even wandered up to the radio booth to do a little color commentating, which became a regular occurrence through the rest of the season.

People with Progeria have a lifespan of about thirteen years. Josiah, though, has already beaten so many odds, and no matter how long he lives, he will long remain with the Spikes. In 2014, State College named an annual team honor after him: the Josiah Viera Perseverance Award.

Meanwhile, Elsewhere in The United States

We focus in this book on minor league teams across the northeast, but the rest of the country is full of ridiculous, hilarious, fantastic team names and logos (and awesome stadiums). Here is just a peak at what exists outside of this handful of states.

Triple A

El Paso Chihuahuas
New Orleans Baby Cakes
Toledo Mud Hens

Double A

Akron RubberDucks
Biloxi Shuckers
Mobile BayBears
Montgomery Biscuits
Pensacola Blue Wahoos
Richmond Flying Squirrels

Single A

Aberdeen IronBirds
Down East Wood Ducks
Everett AquaSox
Fort Wayne TinCaps
Florida Fire Frogs
Tri-City Dust Devils

It's fair to expect that this trend—of cartoonish logos and made-up names only tangentially related to a given town or region—will not slow down. More often than not when a new Biscuits or Baby Cakes is born, merchandise sales blow up. For a lot of teams, those sales and the simultaneous chatter matter.

Acknowledgments

Well, here we are. I wrote a book and had a lot of fun doing so. Some of you might've even read it and had a lot of fun doing so.

It's impossible to express an adequate amount of thanks to those who helped with this project, but let's try.

Thanks to Mark Allison, Amy Lyons, and the rest of the folks at Globe Pequot Press who guided me throughout the process. Mark in particular forever has my gratitude, emailing me out of the blue with a book idea and a question: Did I know anybody who might be interested in writing it? (Spoiler: I did know somebody who was interested in writing it.)

Thanks to the friends and family members who accompanied me to ballparks and ate more stadium food than they otherwise would have—especially my dad, Gerard, for our tour through the boonies of New York and Pennsylvania.

And thanks—a massive thanks—to all the team executives, media relations staffers, photographers, and my fellow sportswriters for their many assists: Michelle Jay, Bill Wanless, Charles Steinberg, Dan Rea, Nate Rowan, Dan Mason, Tim Heiman, Jim Weed, Eddie Saunders, Eric Scarcella, Mike Ventola, Scott Hunsicker, Greg Giombarrese, Chris Tafrow, Chris Cameron, Geoff Iacuessa, Billy Harner, Kevin Mahoney, Terry Byrom, Ashley Grotte, Kevin Kulp, Randy Whitaker, Ian Fontenot, Jane Rogers, Michael Holley, Shawn Smith, Connor Sullivan, Trey Wilson, Paul Stanfield, Joe Doud, Matt Provence, Joe Putnam, Gabe Sinicropi, Kevin Brown, Jason Smorol, Jeff Irizarry, Greg Gania, Dave Schermerhorn, C.J. Knudsen, Josh Olerud, Jeremy Ruby, Todd Hiller, Jon Mozes, Jeff Hurley, David Schofield, Tyler Murray, Jenna Raizes, Chris Chenes, Matt Callahan, Jeff Dooley, Tim Restall, Michael Buczkowski, Brad Bisbing, Travis Sick, Mike Voutsinas, Eben Yager, Greg Joyce, Alex Hall, and Craig Forde.

INDEX

ABOUT THE AUTHOR

TIM HEALEY currently covers the Miami Marlins for the *South Florida Sun Sentinel.* He previously was a writer/editorial producer for the sports website "Sports on Earth," sports correspondent for the *Boston Globe,* and contributor to MLB.com. He also served as associate MLB.com reporter covering the New York Mets. Originally from New England, he now lives near Miami, Florida.

PHOTO CREDITS